East An
by Rail

GW01418167

A guide to the routes, scenery and towns

Jarrold Colour Publications, Norwich

ABOUT THIS BOOK

Originally published in 1984, *East Anglia by Rail* was the pioneer of a series of rail-based guidebooks which now covers practically all Great Britain. Since then, tens of thousands of copies of the fourteen titles in the series have been sold, and have, we hope, shown more people the value of their rail network for exploring all parts of the country.

This third edition of *East Anglia by Rail* brings the information about this fast-growing region and its railways right up to date. The articles are written by local members of the Railway Development Society – the national independent voluntary organisation for rail-users – and its affiliated local rail-users' groups. They know the area well and, as Editor, I am grateful to all of them for their contributions. Thanks are also due to the photographers whose work we have used and to Ruth Clayfield, Shirley Dex, Wendy Lawrence, David Bigg, John Lark and Simon Norton for their help in various ways.

You do not have to be a rail enthusiast to enjoy this book – but some knowledge of railway history and operating will help you to obtain most benefit from it.

The 'up' line or platform is that used by trains to London or another large city; the 'down' line or platform being the opposite. The Great Eastern Railway was the private company formed in 1862, which, with its predecessors, built most of the lines in our region. Its rival in parts of the Fens and Norfolk was the Midland & Great Northern Joint Railway; while the Great Northern Railway Company built the main line from London to Peterborough and beyond, along the western edge of our region, and the majority of the Hitchin to Cambridge route.

A multiple unit, or railcar, is the type of train found on most branches and cross-country lines in East Anglia. 'Sprinter' is the name given to the new generation of diesel multiple units, introduced in the mid-1980s.

The private railway companies were nationalised as British Railways (later British Rail) in 1948. Dr Richard Beeching was Chairman of British Rail in the early 1960s and under his chairmanship many local lines and stations were closed.

Every effort has been made to include up-to-date information. As timetables, fares, entrance times and charges can change at quite short notice, we advise you to check these locally and we have given some addresses and telephone numbers at the back of this guide.

Trevor Garrod
March 1989

© Railway Development Society 1989

Front cover: Norwich-bound Sprinter at Lakenham

Back cover: Norwich Castle, which contains a unique art collection and museum

Title page: Local electric train to Cambridge, near Whittlesford (*Photo:* John C. Baker)

CONTENTS

KEY TO LINE DIAGRAMS

ELY Staffed station; booking-office; train information available; seats and shelter at station.

Beccles Unstaffed station: pay on the train.

WISBECH Served by British Rail bus service.

WANSFORD Preserved station. Open only on certain days; facilities not necessarily available at other times.

Continuous line: no intermediate stations between those shown.

Norwich Through trains from the line shown on the diagram to the destination named.

Broken line: intermediate stations not shown.

L   Ladies' toilet.

G   Gents' toilet.

Ⓘt   Train information board at station.

Ⓘtb   Train and bus information boards at station.

T-FB   Travellers-Fare Buffet.

B   Buffet.

Bks(Dks M-S am) Bookstall (here shown serving take-away drinks Monday to Saturday mornings. Other letters M, F, S, are combined as required).

S   Seats.

Sr   Shelter (waiting-room, or awning, or bus-stop type).

ILFORD Station facilities not shown.

Taxi – Taxi rank at station, or local taxi firm has office at station. L.St. – London (Liverpool Street). K.X. – London (King's Cross). B'ham – Birmingham.

INTRODUCTION

'Cut off from the world by God and the Great Eastern Railway' – that is how one nineteenth-century traveller described East Anglia, that unique region of England bounded east and north by the sea. Boadicea, Edmund, king and martyr, and Hereward the Wake all hailed from this once independent kingdom and staunchly defended it against invaders.

Today, East Anglia remains a distinctive region of historic towns and villages, long breezy coastlines, fens, broads and chalk uplands – but increasing numbers of people are coming to visit and to live and work here. Modern electric trains link all its largest towns and cities to London; while frequent diesel Sprinters provide a through service to most cities of the Midlands and the North, and two major passenger ports attract many tourists from the Continent of Europe. Five hundred and fifty miles of railway serve the counties of Norfolk, Suffolk and Cambridgeshire together with neighbouring parts of Essex, Hertfordshire and Bedfordshire. The train takes you to eight seaside resorts, some big and lively, others small and peaceful; four varied cathedral towns and cities, boating centres, market towns, interesting ports and bustling shopping centres. There are six steam railways or centres (with others planned) and the two largest of these have easy access from the British Rail network.

Whether your interest is in art galleries or first division football; strolling round museums or fishing in sea, lake or river, you will find it in East Anglia. You can admire some splendid medieval churches, explore castles and other ancient monuments from pre-Roman times onward, or you can visit a windmill – and Norfolk has one which can only be reached by boat, on foot – or by train!

The train also lets you view the scenery in a relaxed manner, without the hassle of driving and parking. You will see golden wheatfields, vast fenland vistas, busy broads and estuaries, lonely forest and heath.

East Anglia is not all flat – as a train journey from Ipswich to Beccles, Bishops Stortford to Cambridge, or Norwich to Sheringham will soon reveal. But the hills are not too high and you may well be tempted to explore further from any one of some 120 stations by bicycle. Almost all trains carry cycles, mostly free of charge.

Finally, do not be put off by the estimated cost of your journey. A seven-day Rover or a Day Ranger ticket gives you almost unlimited travel, stopping off whenever and wherever you please, on most of the network. Station staff, British Rail travel agents or the conductor-guard on the train can tell you more about it.

LIVERPOOL STREET–NORWICH
by Steve Hewitt

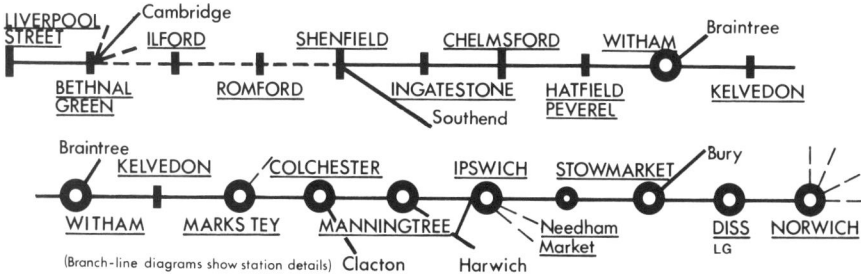

LIVERPOOL STREET — Cambridge — ILFORD — SHENFIELD — CHELMSFORD — WITHAM — Braintree

BETHNAL GREEN — ROMFORD — INGATESTONE — HATFIELD PEVEREL — KELVEDON

Southend

Braintree — KELVEDON — COLCHESTER — IPSWICH — STOWMARKET — Bury

WITHAM — MARKS TEY — MANNINGTREE — Needham Market — DISS — NORWICH

LG

Clacton — Harwich

(Branch-line diagrams show station details)

A journey from London to East Anglia starts from one of the capital's biggest, busiest and, by 1990, one of its most modern termini – Liverpool Street. Built in 1874 to replace the former Shoreditch terminus, Liverpool Street is the gateway to East Anglia. Since 1985, British Rail has undertaken the huge task of modernising the station and restoring it to its former glory. Improvements include better public facilities, better interchange with underground and bus services, and a clear segregation of passenger and parcels traffic. Four million square feet of office space has also been developed – mainly on the former Broad Street station site, but also over the north of Liverpool Street station spanning the approach tracks.

On leaving Liverpool Street, the train slowly crosses the network of tracks that merge from the nineteen platforms, which serve 160,000 passengers daily, into just six lines. (This area was remodelled during 1989 to allow more flexible train movements.) The train ascends to Bethnal Green Junction and gathers speed for its 115-mile run to Norwich.

We soon approach Stratford, with ultra-modern trains of the Docklands Light Railway to be seen to our right. Among a maze of lines to the left, including the important electrified link to the West Coast main line, is the site of the works where the Great Eastern Railway built its locomotives. Soon we speed past rows of terraced houses, 1960s' tower blocks and then suburban semis – Ilford, Romford, Brentwood forming a continuous built-up area – served by frequent electric multiple unit trains in the red, white and blue Network Southeast livery.

The first major town reached is Chelmsford. Many Norwich-bound trains do not stop here, but those that do help to convey commuters back and forth to the capital. The railway crosses Chelmsford on a high embankment and viaduct with views to the left of the premises of Marconi, the electronics firm and the town's largest employer, and to the right, the cathedral and shopping centre.

Leaving Chelmsford, we continue through Springfield, where the Railway Development Society has supported proposals for a new station, and run close to the dual carriageway A12, where the train can race the road traffic. Indeed, along this section of line speeds can touch 100mph as we flash through commuter towns such as Witham and Kelvedon; and soon we see Colchester on its hill to the right.

Colchester has grown steadily since the arrival of the railway in 1843, and is the first main stop for most of the Norwich-bound trains. It is described in an article on page 60. Here you change trains to visit the seaside at Clacton or the charming Stour valley town of Sudbury.

For two decades the overhead electric wires stopped just beyond Colchester. But

5

since 1987 the whole journey to Norwich has been undertaken by electric traction, which has reduced journey times to London to about two hours – or only one hour forty minutes by the crack *East Anglian* express.

Our train presses on to Manningtree, giving us a grandstand view of the Stour valley, immortalised by the great landscape painter, John Constable. Manningtree is well known to rail travellers as the junction for Harwich and the Continent. It is perhaps less well known that a walk of a mile or so from the station, along water meadows, brings us to Flatford Mill, a beauty spot in the heart of Constable country. Nearby lie the pretty villages of East Bergholt, Stratford St Mary and Dedham, whose appeal owe much to their association with Constable.

We pass into Suffolk, climb through the deep Brantham Cutting and speed across hilly country before descending Belstead Bank, approaching Ipswich. On the right, the new Orwell bridge, part of the Ipswich bypass, strides across the estuary. The town's original station was beside the River Orwell until a short tunnel – the only one of this line – was built under Stoke Hill. It is believed to be the first curved tunnel to be built in Britain.

All trains call at Ipswich station, serving the business and commercial centre of Suffolk. Here you can change trains for Felixstowe and Lowestoft, the junction for both lying just beyond the goods yard. The view of Ipswich from the train is of a mixture of modern office blocks and medieval church towers, offset by an interesting-looking former maltings, now a nightclub, just across the river from the station. Ten minutes' walk or a short bus ride brings you into the centre of this thriving, bustling town, described in more detail on page 60.

Leaving Ipswich behind, we now commence the final leg of our journey through some lovely Suffolk countryside. We speed along the Gipping valley and then across flat arable farmland, broken only by the odd cluster of houses whose only remaining link with the railway is a wayside halt, now overgrown and disused. Most of these wayside stations were closed in 1966, but in some of the villages there has recently been pressure to re-open some of them, notably Finningham.

However, we do pass through two quite large communities, the first of which – Stowmarket – is served not only by InterCity trains but also by local Ipswich–Cambridge trains. The station at Stowmarket – a listed building – has been recently refurbished and lies just a few minutes' walk away from the Museum of East Anglian Life, the region's only open-air museum. Re-erected buildings and restored agricultural machinery, craft demonstrations and special events, all illustrate facets of East Anglian life through the centuries.

After Stowmarket we pass Haughley Junction, though all that remains of its station is a signal cabin. Here trains to Cambridge, Peterborough and beyond diverge cross-country. Until 1952, it was also the terminus of the Mid-Suffolk Light Railway from Laxfield. This line was used a great deal during the last war to supply airfields at Mendlesham and Horsham.

Our train speeds on through the village of Mellis, until 1964 the junction for a short branch line to Eye, and on to the town of Diss, after crossing the infant river Waveney. Diss is a thriving community, whose station serves as a railhead for a wide area of north Suffolk and south Norfolk. Sir John Betjeman once described Diss as 'a perfect English market town'. It lies to the west of the station and its character is enhanced by the unusual Mere. The last two decades have seen much new building between the old town centre and the railway; while the station itself has been provided with longer platforms, and since electrification nearly all InterCity trains call there and business has increased substantially.

Lying 2½ miles to the west of Diss on the A1066 Diss to Thetford road is Bressingham Steam Museum and Gardens. It includes a live steam museum, steam-hauled train rides in four gauges over five miles of track, footplate rides

Steam locomotive *Tom Paine* among the trees at Bressingham (*Photo:* Tom Heavyside)

on a main line locomotive and six acres of gardens with 5,000 different species of plants. It is open on varying days during the summer; for further information telephone Bressingham (0379 88) 386. There is no regular public transport to the museum but all the InterCity trains carry cycles free of charge and the road to Bressingham has no hills!

North of Diss we speed across more arable land, through the village of Burston – scene of the famous school strike in 1914, past Tivetshall – junction of the Waveney Valley Railway to Bungay and Beccles, which was closed to passengers in 1953, and past Forncett. In 1881, the Great Eastern Railway built a branch line from here to Wymondham, on the Breckland line, in order to avoid Norwich. But, apart from 1912, when the line north of Norwich was blocked, its potential was never realised and it soon fell into disuse, closing to passengers in 1939.

There are no longer any stations on the twenty-mile stretch between Diss and Norwich, but the Railway Development Society has argued the case for at least one new one, with park-and-ride facilities.

As we approach Norwich, there are views of the attractive Tas valley on the right and Talcolneston television transmitter on the left. Just before reaching Norwich itself, you can observe how big the city has grown, with endless rows of houses broken only by the new cattle market.

We pass over a five-arch viaduct, with the river Yare and Breckland line below, swing right down into the valley and cross the new Trowse swing bridge. Opened in 1987, it is the world's first swing bridge to carry 25kV overhead electric wires, and is situated a few yards upstream from the original 1906 bridge. We then pass Crown Point locomotive and carriage depot on the right. Our journey ends in the six-platform Norwich Thorpe station. Sole survivor of the city's three former termini, it is a gracious building from the 1880s, tastefully refurbished for today's InterCity electrics and a wide range of local and cross-country diesel services.

LONDON–CAMBRIDGE–ELY

by Peter Wakefield

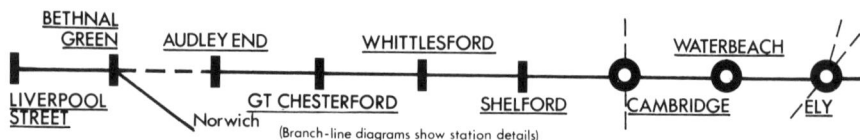

(Branch-line diagrams show station details)

Trains for Cambridge, the Fens and the west of the region leave London from two termini: Liverpool Street and Kings Cross. Both stations have been transformed in recent years so that previous generations would hardly recognise them from the sulphurous caverns they once were. Both stations dispatch at least two electric trains per hour throughout the day to Cambridge.

Liverpool Street is the station most people associate with East Anglia. Trains leaving from there make light work of the incline up to Bethnal Green junction, where they make a sharp left turn to run along the roof-top high viaduct to Hackney Downs. There have been environmental improvements in this part of London, but one can see from the elevated train that a lot remains to be done. At Hackney Downs trains for Cambridge usually make a fork to the right and burrow under Clapton.

A few moments later the train slows again for a sharp left turn off the route to Chingford, and drops down over the Hackney Marshes to join the Lea Valley route from Stratford to Cambridge. It now rapidly gathers speed, rushing through many suburban stations that serve the many thousands of new houses that have been built along the route.

In the Cheshunt and Waltham Cross area little evidence can be seen of the horticulture that was once the basis of the area's prosperity. Houses now sprout where flowers grew. At Cheshunt, the other line from Hackney Downs, via Edmonton, trails in. Some trains to Cambridge use this route. Just over three miles further on, the train stops at Broxbourne, the junction for the Ware and Hertford branch; then on to stops at Harlow Town and Bishops Stortford.

After Bishops Stortford it seems as if London is finally left behind. The train climbs rapidly through rolling chalk country, twisting and turning much more now. The hourly fast trains call only at Audley End and Whittlesford before Cambridge. Another hourly service calls at all stations en route and it is well worth alighting at them. At Stansted, for example, is the small town of Stansted Mountfichet and the interesting reconstruction of a Norman motte and bailey on the site of Mountfichet Castle is hard by the station.

Shortly after leaving Stansted station for Cambridge, a new railway can be seen curving gently away to the east before disappearing from view under the M11 motorway. A few hundred yards further on, a north-facing spur from the new line trails in. The new line will open in 1991 and will take trains nearly three miles to the terminal building of the new Stansted International Airport. The Railway Development Society pressed for the construction of such a link during the marathon Stansted Airport enquiry in the early 1980s.

Just after passing the picturesque village of Newport, expresses, almost without exception, begin to slow for Audley End station, a busy railhead to which the large and always full car-park bears witness. Originally named Wenden, the station, situated in the village of Wendens Ambo, was renamed Audley End seemingly because of its proximity (1½ miles) to the magnificent seventeenth-century mansion of that name. In 1669, the great house was purchased by Charles

8

II and it functioned as a royal residence until 1701. Diminished in size and much altered since then, the mansion is now in the care of the Department of the Environment, and with its gardens bordering the River Cam, is open to the public during the summer.

Audley End station was the junction for Saffron Walden until the closure in 1964 of the branch to that busy market town, 2½ miles distant. Saffron Walden is a place rich in ancient buildings – one of them, the Sun Inn where in 1647 Cromwell had his headquarters. Saffron Walden has various other features worthy of attention, among them the magnificent parish church on an eminence and the largest in Essex, a high street worthy of the name, a spacious tree-bordered common containing the largest earthen maze in England. Another maze, a copy of the famous Hampton Court maze, is part of some extensive and most delightful Dutch-style ornamental gardens in a secluded setting approached through an alley in Castle Street, so named because of the keep and other remains of an early twelfth-century castle nearby. A bus service links Saffron Walden with Audley End station.

The train continues through the two Audley End tunnels and speed is resumed on the downhill run towards Cambridge. From Whittlesford, one of the three stations on this stretch, you can visit the Imperial War Museum at Duxford.

Trains from Kings Cross to Cambridge are now faster than those from Liverpool Street, the hourly fast train calling only at Stevenage. Both routes converge at Shepreth Branch junction, about three miles south of Cambridge station (see page 13 for a description of the route from Stevenage to Cambridge.)

The elegant, refurbished station at Cambridge is unusual because of its very long single through platform. Several million people use it each year, including tourists from all over the world. The city offers many attractions and a useful recent development is a frequent service of open-topped buses to all the main tourist sites from the station forecourt. Cambridge is described in detail on page 59. At present, most trains from London terminate at Cambridge, but frequent connecting services go on to Ely, Peterborough, King's Lynn, Norwich, Newmarket and Bury St Edmunds. After electrification is completed from Cambridge to Ely and King's Lynn, a frequent service of through trains from London will be resumed.

The Fens are reached in the northern suburbs of Cambridge, just before the train speeds over the River Cam at Chesterton Junction. This increasingly industrialised city requires ever more housing and the solitude of the Fens is being breached by more and more people at Milton and Waterbeach, and a new township is planned between Waterbeach and Ely. Two new stations are projected, one on each side of the station at Waterbeach. However, in spite of all this change, the fertile soils of the Fens continue to feed more of our population than any other region.

About fifteen minutes after leaving Cambridge, the busy rail centre of Ely is reached. The station stands by the River Ouse and just at the foot of the hill that leads up to the towering cathedral. Frequent fast trains connect the city with all parts of East Anglia – Peterborough, King's Lynn, Thetford, Norwich, Bury St Edmunds, Ipswich, and Harwich – making it an excellent base from which to tour East Anglia by rail!

PETERBOROUGH–ELY

by Ian Brakewell

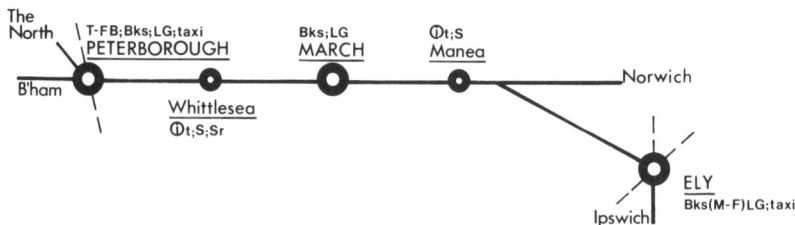

The North | T-FB;Bks;LG;taxi
PETERBOROUGH — MARCH Bks;LG — Manea ①t;S — Norwich
B'ham
Whittlesea ①t;S;Sr
Ipswich — ELY Bks(M-F)LG;taxi

The East Coast Main Line, taking express trains between London and Scotland, could be described as the western boundary of East Anglia, and it is at a point along this line that the visitor must, if travelling farther east, decide to alight. There can be no better place to do this than the thriving, bustling development city of Peterborough, where modern electric trains provide a service to the capital – now less than an hour away. Here, the station and its associated buildings are all modern, redesigned and rebuilt in the 1970s. The city, too, glows with consumer prosperity as shopping centres, pedestrian precincts, and a magnificent cathedral welcome visitors from far afield. Development Corporation grants have enabled Peterborough to create facilities among the best in England: arts and leisure entertainments abound, and for the railway buff there's even a steam railway that chugs westward to Wansford along the valley of the River Nene.

But other delights lie ahead for the unsuspecting traveller. The train connections for East Anglia depart, surprisingly, from the western side of Peterborough station. Our eastbound train simply drops below the level of the old Great Northern main line, and then passes beneath it, curving sharply away to the east as it does so. And here we are in a diesel Sprinter accelerating smartly beyond the site of the old station at Peterborough East and travelling in a direction that is indeed due east.

What sights lie ahead! What an expanse of unending flatness meets the eye! Cambridgeshire is a county that makes eyes ache and hill-lovers despair of seeing rising ground again. Now, as if to emphasise the fact that we are in a new world,

Sprinter 156.415, Blackpool to Ipswich Express near March (*Photo:* John C. Baker)

the brick-pits of King's Dyke gape around us like moon craters. Gaunt chimneys and brick stacks announce our imminent arrival at Whittlesey, first stopping-off place in the Fens.

At Whittlesey, a delightful town with a butter cross, market-place and Church of St Andrew, we witness the first example of railway legend being at variance with local practice. Quite alone now in the district, British Rail persists in spelling the name as 'Whittlesea'. Here we might pause to remark on the number of places on our route whose name ends in 'ea' or 'ey'. Throughout the Fens, this suffix reminds the visitor of the island nature of the region before proper drainage produced the landscape we have today. In Old English, 'ealan' or 'iegland' signified island, and it is said that through appropriate derivation slight rises in the swampy flooded ground were thus suffixed, such as Thorney, Eastrea, Ely (Eel Island). In times of mist and heavy rain, and with treacherous water currents where a king might lose all his treasures at the turn of the tide, such island homes would have been welcome refuges.

As we continue our journey through fields of wheat, barley or beet, where flashing lights at automatic barriers provide the only contrasting colour against a treeless brown and green landscape, the true vastness of the Fens begins to sink in. But surprise is never very far away, and at March, it comes in the most unexpected of guises – a railway centre, or rather, a former railway centre. It doesn't take much stretch of the imagination to look around the seven echoing and largely empty platforms to see again the Victorian glory of this once-proud Great Eastern Railway station. From here, even in the 1960s, it was possible to travel south to St Ives, north to Wisbech, and north-west to Spalding. This last destination lost its direct link as recently as 1982; all that remains now is the east-west connection from Peterborough to Ely – the strategic corridor along which we travel today, the thriving goods link to Wisbech, and the Whitemoor marshalling yards.

The growth of March shows how communities have spread to meet the communication networks that serve them. Nearly three-quarters of a mile south of the station, straddling both sides of the Old River Nene, lies the town's present centre. Here, amid the customary small shops and chain stores of the commercial centre, will be found the charming Nene Parade, the centuries-old Griffin Hotel, and a thriving little market. From the centre, a pleasant riverside path will lead the walker beside weeping willows to the West End town park. This is March (its

etymology shows a link with the 'marches' or border lands between England and Wales), but it is not old March. The original town settlement is yet another mile farther south. Here, way beyond an ancient roadside cross, will be found the parish church of St Wendreda, with its carved double hammer-beam roof, which led Sir Nikolaus Pevsner to declare it to be 'the most splendid timber roof in Cambridgeshire'. Even before this, on a walking tour of the region, the composer Gerald Finzi visited the church and later wrote: 'Looking up at the double hammer-beam roof and the rows of carved angles . . . gave the feeling of a Botticelli Nativity . . . static from the very ecstasy.' But despite this, local wits will doubtless be pleased to point out to you the lone carved devil which can be found amid so many heavenly, winged messengers!

Some Sprinter trains no longer call at March, but even as we slow for the approach to the station we may just catch a glimpse of a freight train taking the west curve into the Whitemoor marshalling yards, or a light engine coming under the Norwood Road bridge from the locomotive depot. The sights, and perhaps a crew-change by the footbridge, serve as reminders of March's railway history. Though much freight-sorting is now done at New England, Peterborough, the cluster of small boys gathered in Norwood Road testifies that there are still sparks of life left in what was once Europe's largest marshalling yard. Skirting the eastern edge of March, the sharp-eyed traveller will be able to discern the former line to Chatteris and St Ives; then his own train heads out once more across miles of deserted fenland.

Between March and Ely, only one station remains open to a handful of local stopping trains, and this is Manea (pronounce it to rhyme with 'rainy'). Here there are a pair of raised platforms and signal-box on the edge of the village. Local people who can remember at first hand the Transport Users' Consultative Committee closure inquiries of the 1960s will tell you that British Rail was not allowed to close Manea on account of the isolated nature of the community it serves. In the event of flooding, the village's uncertain links with the rest of the world were deemed best served by train. Having no eastern access except by train, good sense prevailed, and Manea remains. Its desolation is Cambridgeshire fen at its most typical. Nevertheless, in pre-Beeching years, Manea found company with a handful of evocatively named, equally deserted but enchanting locations. On this line were Stonea and Black Bank; and farther afield Smeeth Road and Middle Drove.

The long straight run to Ely has yet another surprise for us. To see it at its most striking, travel in winter, at night, when there is a full moon. Beyond Manea you will cross the Hundred-Foot Washes which, when in full flood, will produce the illusion of crossing the sea. In its predominant colours of gun-metal grey, silver and black, the ghostly waterscape with reflected moon will combine with the roar of the train wheels on the raised viaduct to make you think you've left land for good on an inexorable run to the edge of the world. What it must have felt like for early travellers we can only imagine, but when the land was expertly drained the five-eighth mile between the Old and New Bedford rivers was left as 'overspill' for the Wash. When this comes, in winter time, the railway is the only crossing place between Mepal and Downham Market.

Now through the sites of two more closed stations, past the storage depot at Chettisham, our train takes us within striking distance of the city of Ely. The cathedral has been visible for some time and suddenly there are tracks all around us, as lines from King's Lynn and Norwich converge at Ely North Junction. The journey, without breaks, takes just over thirty minutes; and in traversing the thirty miles separating Cambridgeshire's two cathedral cities, we have sampled the character and history of the Fens.

HITCHIN–CAMBRIDGE

by Mike Hadley

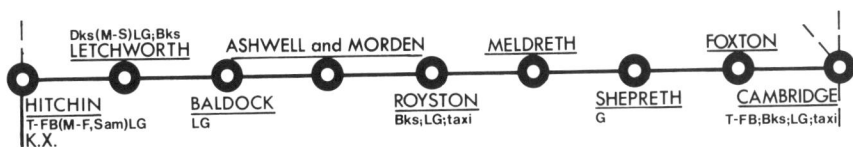

```
    Dks(M-S)LG;Bks
    LETCHWORTH      ASHWELL and MORDEN      MELDRETH          FOXTON
 O──────O──────────O──────────O──────────────O──────────O──────────O──────────O
 HITCHIN          BALDOCK              ROYSTON            SHEPRETH      CAMBRIDGE
 T-FB(M-F,Sam)LG   LG                  Bks;LG;taxi        G             T-FB;Bks;LG;taxi
 K.X.
```

By means of a junction at Hitchin, the rail traveller may gain access to East
Anglia along the 'Great Northern' route to Cambridge. This busy twenty-two mile
line passes through the attractive belt of north Hertfordshire countryside which
gradually gives way to the flatter more rural landscape of Cambridgeshire. Nine
towns and villages are served directly but there are a host of other villages close
by. At one time, the line was to be extended to Oxford, but building did not proceed
west of Hitchin; only the section between Shepreth and Hitchin was specifically
built as part of that cross-country route. Evidence can still be seen of the custom
anticipated at Letchworth, where the station has island platforms for a four-track
layout enabling interchange between trains for London and Oxford. The line offers
considerable scope for holiday-makers and day-trippers with its very attractive
scenery, country walks, pretty villages, the world's first garden city, three market
towns and the magnetic appeal of Cambridge.

Hitchin is a market town, and on Saturdays many bargains may be found
among the stalls set out close to the parish church of St Mary's. At nearby Paynes
Park an interesting collection of paintings and drawings associated with the
town's history may be seen at the museum and art gallery. Shops and public
houses are plentiful and there are several cafés. Various rail trips can be made:
from Hitchin southwards to Stevenage, Hatfield, or down the Hertford line to
Watton at Stone or the county town.

Letchworth Garden city, a few miles north-east of Hitchin, has a host of
attractions and facilities, not least being the city itself with its conservation areas.
There are three trains hourly from London and Royston with connections from
the Peterborough line at Hitchin. Tree-lined avenues, flanked by white pebble-
dash cottages reveal the quality of early town planning. Local information and
guides can be obtained from the Letchworth Shop in Leys Avenue, a two-minute
walk from the station. Here, local crafts can also be obtained. Attractions like the
First Garden City Heritage Museum in Norton Way South and Standalone Farm
should not be missed. Both are within easy walking distance of the centre, the
museum being a three-minute walk from the Letchworth Shop and Standalone
Farm is approximately ten to fifteen minutes walk down Cowslip Hill and Wilbury
Road. The farm is open to the public, all 170 acres catering for visitors and offering
a wide range of livestock and farming equipment, and a wildfowl area with hides
for birdwatching.

Letchworth has a market, hotel, shops, restaurants, sports centre, indoor and
outdoor swimming-pools, a cinema, and a new shopping arcade. A short walk from
the station leads to the common, a natural beauty spot where the famous black
squirrels can be seen. Good rail and bus interchanges can be made with direct
services to Stotfold and Luton, and the coach to and from Oxford sets down close
to the rail station. Keen ramblers will be rewarded if they walk via Norton Way
South to Norton and Norton Bury before ending at Baldock station. This walk of
three miles through town, village and country, can be broken for good food and

drink at the Three Horseshoes in Norton. An evening out in Baldock can easily accommodate all tastes as the town boasts an excellent wine bar and restaurant, a large fish and chip shop and café, high street cafés, and a host of good public houses. Recently, Tesco opened a superstore which has attracted an infux of visitors. There is some interesting architecture here including the church of St Mary's. Walks and cycle trips to surrounding areas must include the villages at Sandon, Radwell and Wallington. The latter village and the farm halfway up the hill were used by George Orwell in his book *Animal Farm*.

Ashwell & Morden station is situated at Odsey but serves the distant villages of Ashwell, Steeple and Guilden Morden. To reach these points, a cycle is ideal. This is a predominantly rural area and is picturesque with its station nestling in a cutting surrounded by fields and a scatter of houses. Two trains hourly in both directions call here and it is an ideal starting point for rambling or cycle rides. The village of Ashwell, two miles away, is charming.

The immediate landscape around Royston is attractive and the town has a market, some interesting back streets and the nearby open spaces of Therfield Heath. The highest point on the Heath affords magnificent views of distant Letchworth and Cambridge as well as over the Bedfordshire countryside. On the Heath, hearty meals can be obtained at the Little Chef on the A505 which skirts the area and runs parallel to the railway into Royston. The Heath is reached by walking from the station (turn right at gates), up into the town until the main crossroads where a right turn is taken. After a few minutes walk the Heath appears on the left. From Royston, an interesting rail tour can be made via Cambridge, Ely, Peterborough, Huntingdon, Hitchin, and back to Royston, perhaps spending a little time at one or two places en route.

After departure from Royston, the first village halt is at Meldreth where a most leisurely way of life is evident. One senses that East Anglia proper has been reached. A visit to Melbourn apples at Meldreth is a must where, in a friendly atmosphere, fresh apples of every kind and other local produce may be obtained. Melbourn and its surroundings have several examples of interesting architecture

King's Cross–Cambridge electric train calls at rural Meldreth (*Photo:* Nick Lewis)

worthy of attention before returning to the station and the train to Shepreth.

No visit to this area would be complete without a call at the crossing keeper's house at Shepreth for a tour of the splendid garden and view of the landscaped railway bank. Walk from the station into the village, taking the first main road to the right back towards the railway. The house and gardens are ahead on the right. Arriving by train, a glance from the window gives an indication of the extent of Mrs Fuller's work with flowers all along the embankment and almost up to the station. A treat for children at Shepreth is Willers Mill Wildlife Sanctuary at the station entrance, where unusual animals can be seen. There is a café here, and this is a Railriders' sticker centre. As an alternative pleasure for the more energetic and those who love attractive villages, thatched roofs and cricket on the green, a walk to Foxton via Barrington is very rewarding, but requires a couple of hours. The public house opposite the green at Barrington is excellent for refreshments.

Finally, no exploration of this area would be complete without a visit to Foxton, but beforehand read *The Common Stream* by Rowland Parker. Described as 'two thousand years of the English village', this book is reputed to reveal more about the history of Foxton than is known about any other village in England. The book is a useful guide on a village walkabout of two or three hours. The villagers are friendly, and their houses are a delight to the eye. A five-minute walk from the station takes one into the village centre and to the church.

After Foxton the train does not stop until Cambridge for connections to other parts of East Anglia. The route is both fascinating and rewarding, with accommodation available at all points from Hitchin to Royston, enabling one to take in the delights of the countryside and enjoy the comforts of the larger towns. Much has had to be left out here, and there is nothing like a visit for thoroughly exploring this area. Be sure to bring along area maps, binoculars, camera, and *British Rail Timetable No. 25*.

All services are operated by electric trains from Hitchin. Two trains each hour serve all stations to Royston and one hourly to Cambridge, Mondays to Saturdays. An hourly service on Sunday calls at all stations along the line to Cambridge. There is usually a trolley service of refreshments on Cambridge trains.

HITCHIN–PETERBOROUGH
by Mike Hadley

T-FB(M-F.S am) LG
HITCHIN
KX

ARLESEY   BIGGLESWADE   SANDY   ST NEOTS   HUNTINGDON
LG taxi

T-FB;Bks;LG taxi
PETERBOROUGH
The North

The forty-four miles of railway from Hitchin to Peterborough form a part of the East Coast main line running from London to Edinburgh. Many record-breaking runs have been made along this line, including the *Mallard* locomotive in 1938 which broke the land speed record. Today express trains such as the *Flying Scotsman*, the *Yorkshire Pullman*, and the *Leeds Executive* can be seen speeding through Hitchin. Indeed, many travellers can be forgiven if they are unfamiliar with the intermediate points along the line as high speed trains pass them so quickly. Predominantly rural, the area surrounding the line between Hitchin and Peterborough is also served by hourly 'all stations' electric trains. The line skirts the western edges of East Anglia serving the communities at Arlesey (a new station opened in 1988), Biggleswade, Sandy, St Neots, Huntingdon and Peterborough.

A mile or so from Hitchin station the line crosses an old Roman road, the Icknield Way, a once busy thoroughfare which is now a narrow but pleasant footpath. It is possible to walk to it from the station via Ickleford village and thence to Letchworth station. Shortly after crossing the Icknield Way, the railway passes alongside England's longest village at Arlesey, famous for its yellow bricks and the 'Blue Lagoon'. The lagoon is disused clay workings which have been admirably disguised by nature's work, and here you can enjoy a picnic and watch inland yachtsmen put their craft through their paces. Arlesey has several pubs and Henlow is only a short walk away from Arlesey station. A walk to the Poppy Hill Farm area is rewarding, offering picnic sites and birdwatching.

Shortly after Arlesey the train passes Langford village and then arrives at Biggleswade. The station is a five-minute walk away from the town centre with some small shops adjacent to the market-place. Overnight accommodation can be obtained at the New Inn or the Crown Hotel in St Andrews Street. The market-place also serves as a bus station with connections to Bedford on no. 176 which runs from next to the central building containing the Market House Restaurant. Food can also be obtained across St Andrews Street along Abbots Walk. A short walk along St Andrews Street leads to the parish church clearly visible from Abbots Walk. By turning left just before the church one can quickly reach Mill Close and the River Ivel. The old mill building has been converted into attractive luxury flats and the bridge gives access to the riverside path and to a children's recreation area. The path along the river is the start of a lovely walk to Sandy, but allow yourself several hours. Stay with the west bank of the Ivel until you reach the A6001 road. Cross the road to the memorial leisure area where the path hugs the east side of the river out into open country. Shortly, the railway line becomes visible in the middle distance to the right. Cross the field, used for grazing cattle, and walk towards a metal railed bridge in front of the railway. Cross the stream on this, following the path to the railway underbridge. Having gone under the railway, keep to the path on the right of the field, which is waymarked Biggleswade Common. The path leads to a little bridge which gives access to Sandy Warren, and the famous BBC transmitter is clearly visible on a hill ahead. The topography changes dramatically as the path starts to climb up Bunkers Hill, crossing the disused and overgrown Oxford to Cambridge Railway, and leads up to Sandy Lodge and the HQ of the Royal Society for the Protection of Birds. Here, there is a choice of either skirting the hill and following the path to the B1042 road to Sandy station or going up the hill and joining the road at the top.

Sandy Lodge and the RSPB are the chief attractions at Sandy and whilst they are open to the public it is advisable to check for days and hours of opening. Sandy station is well situated for those with a bicycle as Bedford can be reached in approximately thirty minutes. For the energetic cyclist, a circular trip can be made taking in Potton, Wrestlingworth, Guilden Morden and Steeple Morden in an easterly direction ending up at Ashwell station on the Cambridge line.

After Sandy, the train calls at St Neots where more riverside walks can be made. This is a market town with some impressive old brewery buildings. Compared to Sandy, St Neots seems large, with pubs, shops, and plenty of places to eat. Set on the River Great Ouse, which meanders from Bedford to Ely, St Neots enjoys a river-bus service to Bedford at certain times of the year. The station is about fifteen minutes walk from the centre and riverside, but for the cyclist, is the start

of a fine circular ride by way of Staughton Green to West Perry and Grafham Water and on via Buckden, Offord Darcy and Great Paxton and back to St Neots.

Seven miles further north the train again calls at Huntingdon which has plenty to attract the visitor. There are associations with Oliver Cromwell and Samuel Pepys lived at nearby Brampton. There are museums, shops and restaurants with more riverside walks, with perhaps a visit to Godmanchester, a beautiful and very English village. Finally, no visit to Huntingdon would be complete without cycling to the village of Buckden with its palace, en route to Grafham Water and its bird reserves. From Grafham one can cycle south and rejoin the railway at St Neots. There are buses to St Ives, Cambridge or Bedford (also serving some attractive Ouse Valley villages). There is an infrequent bus service to Ramsay and the National Trust Abbey Gatehouse.

There are no stations between Huntingdon and Peterborough and to explore this area a good bicycle is useful. The area is rural and simply being there in the fresh air is enough to create that feeling of 'getting away from it all'. Connections to most parts are good via Peterborough interchange station, and the city is a good base for a stay in this area with hotels, guest-houses and a camp site along the Nene Valley. An indoor shopping centre, cathedral, and the Nene Valley Railway make Peterborough ideal for a day out in itself.

NENE VALLEY STEAM RAILWAY
by John Goose

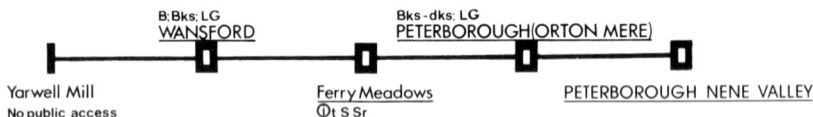

B:Bks; LG
WANSFORD

Bks-dks; LG
PETERBOROUGH(ORTON MERE)

Yarwell Mill
No public access

Ferry Meadows
①t S Sr

PETERBOROUGH NENE VALLEY

Peterborough's first railway, opened on 2 June 1845, ran along the Nene Valley to Northampton. British Rail closed the route to passengers in 1964 and to freight in 1972; but total closure was short-lived, for from 1 June 1977 a passenger timetable again operated from Orton Mere, on the edge of the city, to Wansford. The Peterborough Railway Society had persuaded the city's Development Corporation to purchase six miles of trackbed so that a steam railway could enhance the Nene Park Leisure Area.

Wansford Station, by the A1 road at Stibbington, became the railway's headquarters. The main building is from nearby Barnwell and has been reconstructed. There is a small turntable, an attractive footbridge, locomotive sheds, a museum, a shop, refreshment carriages, and the longest fully equipped preserved signal-box in Britain on the site. Many of the score of steam locomotives, as many carriages, and half a dozen diesels to be seen are of continental origin, for uniquely in Britain the line operates to the Berne loading gauge. British locomotives usually present are the Class 5 *City of Peterborough*, 'Battle of Britain' *92 Squadron*, and a tank engine officially named by the Reverend W. Awdry as *Thomas*.

Since September 1983 journeys westward beneath the A1 and through the 616-yard-long Wansford Tunnel have become possible to Yarwell Mill, an attractive stretch of the Nene with its water-mill, touring caravan park, and flooded excavation pits. Here there is no public access and our locomotive must run round at

Token change at Wansford, Nene Valley Railway (*Photo:* C. Pinion)

the old junction of the routes from Northampton and Rugby, the nearby bridges having been removed on both.

Eastwards from Wansford, the Nene lies south of the railway, and the trackbed of the old Stamford and Essendine branch closed in 1931 curves away to the north. Soon the site of Castor Station, perhaps a later rebuilding project, appears and opposite, beyond the river, the village of Water Newton with, farther on, the site of Durrobrivae, a Roman town which straddled Ermine Street. On crossing the Nene one then enters the centrepiece of this whole amenity area, Ferry Meadows Country Park. Based on attractive lakes in a curve of the river, it offers every imaginable water sport and pastime, nature reserves, riding, caravanning, golf, a trim track, adventure playgrounds, a miniature railway, an information centre and café, and extensive walks. Ferry Meadows Station with its interesting platform murals stands at the park entrance.

Eventually the railway runs close by the river at Orton Staunch with its lockgate and pleasure craft. Here Orton Mere Station, a new brick building in traditional style and with sales facilities, is accompanied by a signal-cabin and passing-loop. Parallel tracks leave the station beneath a massive road bridge and continue as far as Longueville Junction, where one route turns south to link with British Rail's Fletton Loop from the main line to the nearby sugar-beet factory. British Rail has run diesel multiple units along this route on summer Saturdays to link Peterborough mainline station with the Nene Valley Railway.

Now, however, the steam railway has its own route leading close to the heart of the city. The other tracks from Longueville Junction continue eastwards beside the Nene for a further 1½ miles to where the route once joined the Peterborough–March line beneath the main line. No connection is contemplated here, but close by, on the site of the former London & North Western Railway engine shed, stands the new Peterborough Nene Valley Station. The station site is still being developed, but was officially opened for public use with the final 1½ miles of track extension by HRH Prince Edward on 30 June 1986. This station development, eventually with full facilities, only a few minutes walk from the city centre, with more land available and with ready access from the spacious Oundle Road carpark in Fair Meadow, offers exciting prospects for further railway activity. The organisation Railworld has established an office on the site to plan its Museum of World Railways which, it is hoped, may one day emulate and complement the National Railway Museum at York.

18

ELY–KING'S LYNN

by Chris Milnes

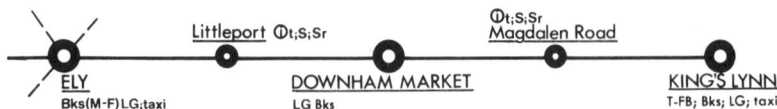

Littleport $①$t;S;Sr

$①$t;S;Sr
Magdalen Road

ELY
Bks(M-F)LG;taxi

DOWNHAM MARKET
LG Bks

KING'S LYNN
T-FB; Bks; LG; taxi

(NB Magdalen Road is to be renamed Watlington)

The twenty-six mile Ely to King's Lynn railway has recently been incorporated into Network SouthEast, the largest passenger operation on British Rail, covering all the London commuter services and several longer distance semi-InterCity lines. King's Lynn is one of the furthest points of the Network SouthEast empire!

The two-hourly train service is formed of 'Mk2', and sometimes 'Mk3' carriages, hauled by Class 47 locomotives. Several vehicles have been refurbished internally and painted in Network SouthEast livery. A benefit of this coaching stock is that there is plenty of van space for luggage, prams, and bicycles, an important asset for cyclists touring in this flat part of the country. Most trains have a mini-buffet facility for snacks and drinks. Future plans may include 'modular catering' on some trains, which should enable a greater range of meals to be served.

We begin our journey at Ely, a three-platformed station. The buildings have received some light renovation work, and there have been some alterations to track and signals. As we pull out of Ely, on the left is a picturesque marina and the large Maltings, now used as a meeting place, with the cathedral dominating the skyline. After the marina, we pass, on the left, flooded gravel workings, now a small bird sanctuary. At Ely North junction the line branches into three – one to March, one to Norwich and the middle one to King's Lynn. The large industrial building on the right, formerly a British Sugar refinery, is now used as a privately owned freight distribution depot, handling many rail-borne cargoes such as rock salt and lime.

Beyond the junction we head out across slightly undulating farmland for about five miles until a caravan site next to the river heralds our arrival at Littleport. We pass over Sandhills level crossing, and a quarter of a mile further on reach Littleport station, an unstaffed halt. The village centre is about one mile away on the left. Near the station is a boatyard and a small restaurant. North of Littleport, as the railway becomes single track, we pass the recently opened Littleport by-pass, and pick up speed to a maximum 75 mph. The countryside becomes flatter and the soil blacker – typical Fen country. We pass the sites of Black Horse Drove and Southery public goods' sidings, closed in 1964 – all that remains of them to the observant traveller, is a concrete pathway, and old railway fencing set further back from the line, indicating that there was activity there long ago.

Two miles on, at Hilgay, an automatic level crossing over a single track road and a concrete hut are all that remains of the station axed in 1964. About a mile further on, our train slows to a 20 mph subsidence speed restriction over the bridge crossing the River Great Ouse. Subsidence is a great problem for fenland railways, caused by peat drying out and shrinking in dry weather and then swelling in wet weather. In this case the embankment has slipped; other stretches of our line have been relaid with deep limestone ballast to improve track stability. We accelerate and approach Denver junction where railway cottages and remains of a platform tell us that, here too, there was once a station. The branch line to

Stoke Ferry used to join our line on the right, but was closed to passengers in 1930. Freight delivery to the Wissington sugar refinery ended by 1981, the line being unable to accept heavy modern freight rolling-stock.

After Denver comes Downham Market, a small town whose attractive station building is of carstone, a local material like sandstone. Over the years the local Amenity Society has improved the station with shrubs, baskets and even new station signs. A short walk away is the town centre with a small shopping arcade, some pleasant pubs and hotels, and an attractive black and white clock tower. North from Downham Market the line runs alongside the Great Ouse, which is behind the large bank on our left. Stow Gate box marks the site of a small station serving Stow Bardolph, another 1964 casualty. After passing Holme Road level crossing our train slows for Magdalen Road station, serving Watlington to the east and Wiggenhall St Mary Magdalen to the west. This station was closed in 1968, but reopened after a campaign by local people in 1975. Money was raised and new lighting installed. Now new houses are springing up around the station, and it will have an increasing role to play in future.

Five miles beyond Magdalen, we approach King's Lynn. At Harbour Junction lines branch off to serve Campbell's Soups, the British Sugar refinery and Dalgety grain and fertiliser plant. The large silos on the left belong to a brand new grain depot built on the site of the old South Lynn goods yard. Our train slows as we pass over Extons Road open crossing and past redundant sidings, allotments and houses backing onto the line. At Tennyson Avenue level crossing, note on the right a single-track line trailing in from the British Industrial sand quarry at

Ely cathedral

Middleton Towers, about three miles away. This line once went to Dereham.

We are now drawing into the station, which was a fairly spacious terminus, but only two of the five platforms are now used for passenger trains. Until 1969, local rail services operated from King's Lynn to Hunstanton, Norwich via Dereham and to Wisbech. The services were formed of efficient and reliable diesel railcar sets, and were popular with shoppers and holiday-makers. Unfortunately, under the tail-end period of the Beeching regime, the lines were all closed – the last one to Hunstanton on 5 May 1969. These closures have left King's Lynn with a legacy of heavily congested and dangerous local roads. Often a five mile car journey into town can take as much as forty minutes, despite the town being by-passed in all directions! Part of the railway to Hunstanton will live on though, helped by the railway's ally, the bicycle, as part of the track bed is to become a cycle track.

Although the local passenger services have gone, freight continues to flourish with much new traffic. The main operation is the movement of 250,000 tonnes per year of white silica sand to Yorkshire for glass-making. The sugar refinery receives limestone and oil, and grain and fertiliser are also transported in large quantities. Imported steel is railed to the West Midlands, and petroleum coke dispatched to Cambridge. Canned food goes to Scotland on Speedlink fast freight services, and other goods handled include chemicals and timber, and occasionally container trains when other ports are disrupted by strikes.

The station itself is of interest, having been built in 1847, and has recently benefited from an extensive refurbishing programme. The buffet is one of few to remain of the old style and has been improved extensively.

The town centre is only a quarter of a mile to the west of the station. Be careful, though, when crossing the two busy roads to the centre, as there is no pedestrian crossing on either. The shopping centre has many large chain stores, plus several smaller shops. Adjacent to the station is a large Texas Homecare superstore. The busy town also contains many interesting old buildings and the Tuesday market-place is attractive. Several of the old quayside buildings have been renovated, and there are many interesting side streets and river banks, often crowded with small fishing boats, to investigate. Part of the river front was used recently as a film set for *Revolution*, in which the river was made to look like New York in 1790, and old sailing ships were brought in. King's Lynn also has many interesting pubs; for real ale freaks there are currently twelve different real ales available in the town.

Not far from the railway station is the bus and coach station. There are frequent bus services on the scenic routes to Hunstanton via Sandringham. Castle Rising, about three miles from King's Lynn, is also well worth a visit. In the summer, Eastern Counties run a Norfolk Coastliner bus service, twice a day, three days a week from King's Lynn along the coast to Yarmouth. This provides access to many attractive places, like Brancaster Staithe (for the ferry to Scolt Head Island), Holkham (for the Hall), Wells-next-the-Sea (with its two narrow gauge railways), Blakeney and Sheringham.

In February 1989, the Secretary of State for Transport approved the electrification of the line from Cambridge to King's Lynn at a total cost of £20,100,000 including new rolling-stock. Work should be complete by the end of 1991, when the growing population of West Norfolk will then be at well under two hours' travelling time from the capital. Much of the credit for the successful campaign to electrify this line must go to King's Lynn & West Norfolk Borough Council, which produced a wealth of well-researched material showing the benefits of an electric rail link and which, with Norfolk County Council, has offered up to £750,000 operating subsidy over six years to the new electric service, should such finance be needed.

PETERBOROUGH–KING'S LYNN RAIL LINK COACH

by John Goose

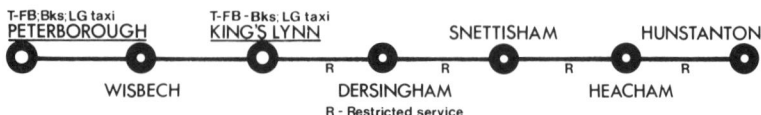

Since 17 May 1982, holders of rail tickets to King's Lynn have, for certain journeys each day, found themselves leaving Peterborough Station from its 'extra platform' on the forecourt, There, under the shadow of the impressive and much enlarged Great Northern Hotel, we are confronted by a modern motor coach which, with its red, white and grey livery and British Rail logo, appears to be striving to look like a train. As well as serving Wisbech and King's Lynn, the coach now also runs once daily (twice on Saturdays) through to the coastal resort of Hunstanton.

After passing out of Peterborough and through the village of Eye, the journey continues across the level Fens on the long, straight roads made possible by the chequered field patterns of this flat landscape. The equally straight course of the former Midland and Great Northern Joint Railway, closed to passengers in 1959 and a few years later to freight, can be seen at times running to the north of the road, as if it were a ghost from the past. The first request stop is made at Thorney, an old estate village built by the Dukes of Bedford.

At Guyhirn, we cross the route of the former March–Spalding line (closed in November 1982) near to where we pass over the River Nene, before following its banks to Wisbech.

Wisbech is served by rail with the branch from March carrying an encouraging amount of freight. This is now mainly pet foods to and from the Spillers terminal, formerly the Eastern Goods Yard, but also there is movement of metal waste and sometimes steel coil and engineering products. The passenger service ceased in 1968, but since 1978 six successful passenger excursions have been run on the initiative of the Railway Development Society, carrying local people to Cambridge for shopping (three times) and to the seaside resorts of Lowestoft, Felixstowe and Scarborough.

With their Rail Link Coach service British Rail would seem to be conceding that Wisbech has a large enough population to warrant a rail link (no larger town in East Anglia is without one); or, at least, that a more direct east-west route from North Norfolk to Peterborough, the Midlands and the North should have been retained.

Wisbech has many notable buildings, including the magnificent Georgian Brinks alongside the river, Elgoods Brewery, Peckover House (built in 1722 for a local banking family and now a Grade 1 listed building, open to the public by the National Trust), the old grammar school, Gilbert Scott's seventy-foot-high Clarkson Memorial and the Crescent area with its oval of Georgian town houses on the site of the former castle. The museum, parish church, inns and markets are all worth a visit.

Our coach then heads towards King's Lynn and is soon again among flat arable fields, but in perhaps a rather more mature landscape where the road is, at times, not so straight, some of the houses are more ancient, and the countryside is dotted with fine medieval churches.

The decorative Customs House on the quay at King's Lynn

As we approach the River Great Ouse the large tanks and towers of the King's Lynn sugar-beet factory can be seen on the far bank. We cross the river on a new bridge virtually where the old Midland and Great Northern Joint Railway bridge once stood. Storage sidings for the beet factory and grain silos stand close by on the right where South Lynn Station used to be – this freight spur being one of the few short stretches of the M & GN still in use.

When we begin to thread our way through the streets of the ancient and venerable port of King's Lynn as if to emphasise the town's past grandeur, we still must pass through the South Gate, built not for defence, but in 1440 as an example of civic pride. Two sharp turns to the right from the main streets bring us into the forecourt of King's Lynn railway station and again in touch with the British Rail passenger network. Two hostelries across the street, the Greyfriars and the East Anglian Hotel (the later still proudly proclaiming itself a 'posting establishment'), welcome the weary Rail Link Coach traveller; one thing our coach could not provide in its strenuous efforts to be a train of the road was a buffet!

The restricted service beyond King's Lynn presents the traveller with a very different scene: rolling and often wooded countryside. We pass near to the Queen's residence of Sandringham House and its impressive former royal station at Wolferton, and then, after stops at the attractive villages of Dersingham, Snettisham and Heacham, we reach the thriving little seaside town of Hunstanton. British Rail has wisely now resumed a service to this resort which lost its railway in May 1969; for with a fairground, sports leisure complex and caravans at one end and gardens, the attractive green, bowling, golf, and yachting at the other, plus excellent beaches, Hunstanton indeed has a wide appeal to visitors of many different tastes.

ST EDMUNDS LINE

by John Brodribb

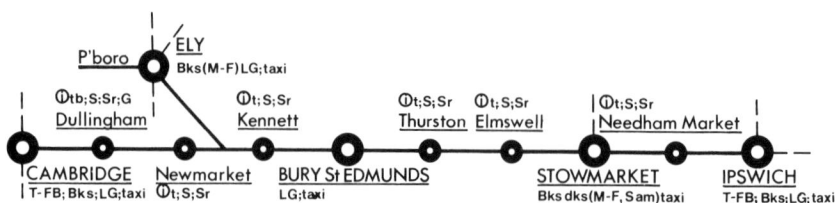

P'boro — ELY Bks(M-F)LG;taxi — Dullingham ⓞtb;S;Sr;G — Kennett ⓞt;S;Sr — Thurston ⓞt;S;Sr — Elmswell ⓞt;S;Sr — Needham Market ⓞt;S;Sr — CAMBRIDGE T-FB;Bks;LG;taxi — Newmarket ⓞt;S;Sr — BURY St EDMUNDS LG;taxi — STOWMARKET Bks dks(M-F, Sam)taxi — IPSWICH T-FB;Bks;LG;taxi

The St Edmunds line of British Rail joins several important towns, notably Cambridge, Ely, Bury St Edmunds, Newmarket, Stowmarket and Ipswich, and serves a number of smaller communities as well. In addition to local services, the route, opened between 1846 and 1854, also carries many through services between East Anglia, the Midlands, and the north-west. Many connections are available at Peterborough.

Cambridge station is some distance from the city centre, although there is a frequent bus service between the two. The attractions of Cambridge are considerable, and whilst many visitors come to see the colleges, there are several other buildings of architectural interest. It has many excellent shops and restaurants, as well as a fine cricket ground in Fenners. There is a good street plan in the station booking-hall, and though the travel centre sells the official guide, it is worth going to the tourist office off Market Hill for a very good range of maps and guides. Cambridge station is unusual in having only one long platform serving trains in both directions, although there are bay platforms at both ends for local services. St Edmunds line trains usually leave from one of these at the north end, soon diverging sharply from the main line in an easterly direction.

After clearing the suburbs of Cambridge, the line climbs to pass the site of Fulbourn station, and traverses open arable country before woodland heralds the approach to Dullingham station, some eleven miles out. It is a quiet spot, and the traveller alighting here can watch the train disappear into the distance while the signalman closes the level-crossing gates behind it. The village is about ten minutes' walk along the lane, and a further ten minutes' stroll, past the grounds of Dullingham House, brings the church, village green and two pubs into view.

The train traveller will now be in Newmarket, a pleasant town famed as the home of the Jockey Club and Britain's main centre for the 'sport of kings'. The station building, a vast and splendid red brick structure, is now used by a local company supplying the needs of horse-racing, and trains use the one remaining platform. The town centre is reached by turning right out of the station and left at the end of the road; Tattersall's sales paddocks are on the way. There is a town map on the right as one enters the High Street, and a little further along is the National Horseracing Museum, a 'must' for anyone interested in the Turf.

On leaving Newmarket, the train passes grain sidings and plunges into Warren Hill tunnel (the longest in East Anglia) before emerging into deeply wooded surroundings. At Chippenham Junction the line from Ely joins from the left, and on the right racehorses can often be seen exercising. The A45 trunk road appears on the left, and from now on keeps very close company with the train. Five miles from Newmarket is Kennett station, serving the villages of Kennett and Kennett End. The weary traveller will find the Bell free house within ten minutes' walk – turn right out of the station. Still in close company with the A45, the line passes two small closed stations, one of which, Saxham & Risby (closed in 1967), is the

24

site of a large agricultural machinery depot. At length, twenty-nine miles from Cambridge, the train pulls into Bury St Edmunds. The large station betrays a much busier past; branch lines once diverged to both north and south.

There is much to see in Bury. The town centre is about twenty minutes' walk: turn right out of the station drive and keep more or less straight on. Turn right at the lights; this will bring you out at Angel Corner with its National Trust Clock and Watch exhibition. Alternatively, go straight ahead out of the station up the slope, and again keep going roughly in the same direction when you get to the road. You will pass the famous Rollerbury skating centre; bear right at the bottom of the hill and left at the next junction and you will again come to the town centre, passing the Central Library on your left.

Trains continue from Bury St Edmunds station, crossing over the main Thetford road and the A45. Seven minutes' ride away is Thurston station; the platforms are on a high embankment and a pub for refreshment is clearly visible below.

Birmingham–Harwich Sprinter passes through Thurston on a summer afternoon (*Photo:* John C. Baker)

The impressive building is now occupied by a printing firm, that on the other platform having been demolished some years ago. Considerable housing developments have taken place here in recent years, some of which can be seen from the railway. It is a pleasant walk through the lanes to Elmswell, passing through the unspoilt village of Tostock, and although much of the countryside has been denuded of trees and hedges in the name of agricultural efficiency, there still remain some pleasantly wooded parts.

Elmswell station is a further seven minutes' ride from Thurston and serves a large village with pub and shops immediately by the station. It is also good cycling country, but beware of the restrictions on bikes on the Sprinter cross-country trains. The railway continues on its undulating course for a further $3\frac{1}{2}$ miles before trains slow for Haughley Junction, where they join the main Norwich to Ipswich line.

All trains from Ely and Cambridge stop at the next station, Stowmarket, an elaborate 1846 edifice with ornate gables and considerable amounts of decorative brickwork and other embellishments. When electrification of the main line was in progress, the platform canopies had to be cut back to provide extra clearance for the overhead wires, and British Rail took great care that the new work blended with the old: the station building now enjoys listed status. As with other stations, much of the redundant land formerly in use as a goods yard has been turned over to car-parking and a bus interchange, provided in cooperation with the local authority.

There is one more stop before Ipswich at Needham Market. This station was closed in 1967, along with all the other stations between Ipswich and Norwich except Stowmarket and Diss. It reopened in 1971 and local trains to Cambridge call there; it also enjoys a through electric connection with Liverpool Street morning and evening. Ipswich is about ten minutes away, with some cross-country trains now continuing to Harwich or even Colchester. This last section of the route runs parallel to the Gipping Valley River Path, which connects Ipswich and Stowmarket and mostly follows the towpath of the erstwhile Stowmarket Navigation. It can be reached in a number of places, and is accessible by going along Princes Street, opposite Ipswich station, and following the public footpath sign after crossing the River Gipping. The County Council has erected a number of information boards along the route; Bramford is a particularly pleasant spot for a picnic.

Travellers from the Midlands and north will arrive on the St Edmunds line via Ely, taking advantage of the greatly-improved Sprinter Express service. The section between Ely and Chippenham Junction (near Newmarket) is very different from the other parts. Leaving Ely in a southerly direction, Ipswich trains diverge almost at once from the main line, climbing to cross the River Great Ouse. Black fenland soil stretches away on both sides of the line, and supports a variety of crops such as carrots or onions. Trains do not stop until Bury, but the site of Soham station, about five miles from Ely where the line goes from single to double, is fairly clear. It was the scene of remarkable heroism one night in June 1944 when the front wagon of a loaded ammunition train caught fire. Driver Benjamin Gimbert and fireman James Nightall uncoupled the blazing vehicle and tried to get it clear of the station; but it exploded, killing the fireman and the signalman on duty, and badly injuring driver Gimbert. However, their courageous act saved the town from almost certain destruction and they were awarded the George Cross.

Continuing towards Bury, the large Snailwell scrapyard on the left precedes the Snailwell stud farm, where racehorses can often be seen exercising. Chippenham Junction is soon passed, the line from Newmarket trailing in from the right.

BRECKLAND LINE
by Gordon Knott

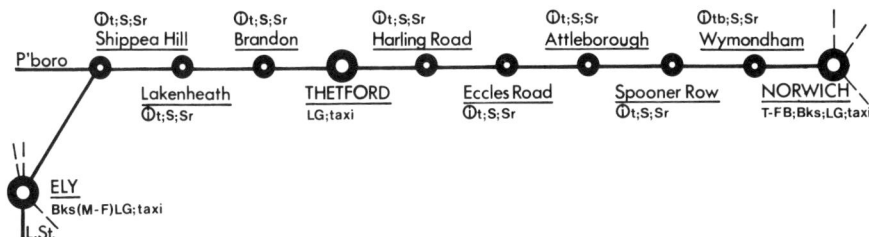

If you have made your way by train from Cambridge or Peterborough, by the time you reach Ely, you will have begun to wonder whether the scenery – a vast expanse of flat fenland – will ever change. If you take the Breckland line, it will have changed – not once, but several times and interestingly – and your trip will reward you. The line is now served by the new Sprinter trains, at roughly hourly intervals, between Norwich, Thetford, Ely, Birmingham and Liverpool, as well as by local stopping trains. Sprinter speeds are higher, and comfort rather greater, but beware of summer Saturdays, when trains can be uncomfortably or impossibly full.

Swinging away from Ely, you leave its grand cathedral and its boats on your left. After reflecting perhaps for a moment how those medieval men brought all that stone to a hill in the middle of a huge marsh, watch the lines to Peterborough and King's Lynn vanish to your left, and ride once more through the open fen with seemingly more celery than the world could possible eat on either side. Look out for the otherwise unromantic fenman's habit of growing masses of flowers round his house, and numbers of pheasants which seem to ignore the passing trains, and before you know it you are at Shippea Hill. (What hill? You may well ask. In fact, the '-ea' at the end of the name, not unusual round here, indicates one of the old islands that stood up from the Fens.)

From this staging-point for many Americans on their way to the great bases at Lakenheath and Mildenhall, you can make your way by foot or cycle (but don't expect to find a bus!) to either of these places, with their fine angel-roofed churches. If you stay on the train, in five miles you will reach Lakenheath station. On for another five minutes to Brandon, and as you go the scenery begins to change for the first time. On your left, the River Little Ouse comes alongside, and from being little more than a fenland dyke becomes a real river of the kind that country-lovers expect, and smaller fields take over from the great fenland plain.

At Brandon comes the second change, and you enter the Breckland from which the line takes its name. Once a great dustbowl created by the foolish farming ways of our prehistoric ancestors, it became a vast heath covering many square miles, on which little grew except heather and scrub. Modern farming has now recovered much of it, and the Forestry Commission with Thetford Forest have changed the face of that part which you are now entering.

Brandon itself is a pleasant, unpretentious Suffolk town with a number of good pubs. From here you can explore the forest which stretches for miles, follow the river to the beautifully set village of Santon Downham (but the best view of all is possibly from the train), or visit Grime's Graves, from which prehistoric men dug out flints for their implements.

InterCity train on the Breckland line passing through Thetford Forest (*Photo:* John C. Baker)

It is seven miles to Thetford if you choose to walk or cycle (and the whole of the Breckland line runs through ideal cycling country, with few steep hills and many pleasant lanes), but the train will take you there in ten minutes or so. Before you leave the station, look at the unusual ironwork on the pillars supporting the platform awnings, with their railway motif. The largest town on the line, Thetford, is an Inter-City stop, and all fast trains to Norwich and Birmingham, as well as some summer holiday trains to Great Yarmouth, call here.

With its large London overspill estates and its new industries, Thetford has seen much change, but it is a town of great antiquity and well worth a visit. Its castle mound and priory and abbey ruins can easily be visited on foot, as can its shopping centre and pleasant riverside walks by the Little Ouse and Thet. There are several hotels in the town, and camping sites in the forest for the walker and cyclist. While you are there, don't forget to visit Kilverstone Wildlife Park, with its miniature studs, a mile and a half from the station in a beautiful woodland setting and a treat for the children.

On from Thetford through the forest again, and in about five minutes you will be crossing Roundham Heath and catch a glimpse of the Breckland that was, with heather, bracken, and scrub, on your way to Harling Road, a mile from the village of East Harling, which has a fine church and a pleasant little market-place with old houses. As you leave the heath the countryside undergoes its third change, and you enter the slightly rolling landscape of fields and trees typical of so much of Norfolk. Eccles Road station serves the hamlets of Eccles and Quidenham, with their interesting little round-towered churches, of which Norfolk has so many. These bear witness to the inability of small parishes to pay the cost of importing stone and their manner of using local flint (which cannot be cut square) to the best advantage.

Between Harling Road and Eccles Road, look out on your left for cars and motor cycles speeding round the Snetterton Racing Circuit (meetings from March until the end of October, at weekends). The short branch across the fields to grain silos, just before you reach Eccles Road station, was opened with the help of a government grant on 10 July 1985.

Attleborough is a small town on the main road from London to Norwich and has grown rapidly in recent years. Apart from the solid, squat parish church and the Griffin pub, it contains few buildings of great note, but as you enter the station look out for the huge piles of kegs and barrels which signal the large cider factory for which the town is known.

At Banham, some five miles from Attleborough (once more, don't expect to find a bus) you may sample many kinds of cider and local wines at a cider house, or visit Banham Zoo, a well laid out local attraction.

It is quiet but pleasant country now all the way; and after passing Spooner Row, the smallest station on the line, look out on your left for the oddly assorted twin towers of Wymondham Abbey. Wymondham ('Windham' to the locals if you are asking for a ticket) is an attractive town, with narrow streets full of old houses, and a fine seventeenth-century market cross; it has a number of good shops and pubs and a visit to the town and abbey will repay the effort.

The freight-only line from Dereham (closed to passengers in 1969 but used by some twenty excursion trains operated by the Railway Development Society and the Wymondham–Dereham Rail Action Committee since 1978) trails in from the left. At the time of writing it is threatened with total closure. Wymondham station buildings have recently been lovingly restored by a local businessman, who is opening a tea-room and piano showroom in them; they merit more than a casual glance from the traveller.

You are now on the final stage of you journey to Norwich, the 'fine city' of which Cobbett wrote and of which its people are justly proud. As your train speeds down from Hethersett, do not miss Keswick water-mill on your right, just after you have crossed the River Yare for the first time. On down this small valley, your train runs through the water-meadows and under Harford viaduct, which carries the main line from London; it drops down and joins the Breckland line just before the now disused Trowse station. A swing bridge takes you over the River Wensum and you may catch, if you are lucky, a sight of one of the small coasters which still come up to Norwich from the sea. Norwich itself, with its infinite variety of things to do and see, then awaits you.

BROADS LINE
by Wallace Boyles

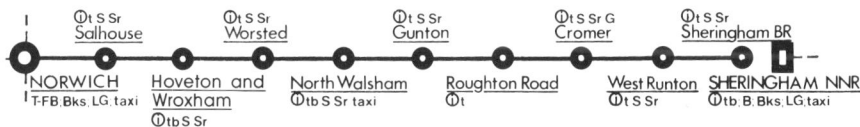

Norfolk is noted among other things for its profusion of churches – some of them 'pocket cathedrals' situated in tiny villages and small towns reflecting the county's medieval prosperity and wealth – and a series of shallow lakes known as 'Broads'. These are water-filled excavations abandoned by late Saxon and early medieval peat diggers and together with the connecting rivers afford some 200 miles of navigable waters and attract thousands of tourists year after year.

The Broads, which in 1988 acquired the status of a national park, are centred mainly on three rivers: the Yare, which empties into the sea at Great Yarmouth, the Waveney (partly in Suffolk), and the Bure; the two latter joining the Yare within a short distance of Great Yarmouth.

The most important of the three confluent rivers, from the standpoint of the Broads, is the Bure, which, fed by its tributaries the Ant and the Thurne, at one

On the River Bure at Wroxham

point in its fifty-eight mile course forms the boundary between two villages, Hoveton and Wroxham, the latter long regarded as the most notable and popular of the Broadland centres – the 'capital of the Broads'. The neighbouring villages, connected by an ancient humpback bridge reinforced today by a steel truss, are served by the line from Norwich to the resorts of Cromer and Sheringham, and it is this route which has been named the 'Broads line'.

Broads line trains leave the Wherry line 1¾ miles out of Norwich at Whitlingham Junction and begin an initially steep ascent out of the Yare Valley, eventually to level out for a steady run to Salhouse, four miles distant. On the way we pass through the expanded village of Rackheath, whose inhabitants for many years have yearned for a halt and who, wistfully perhaps, hear our klaxon as we approach the three automatic level crossings in the vicinity. A coal dump visible in the distance on the left of the isolated station serving the scattered village of Salhouse, marks the site of a large wartime bomber aerodrome of which little now remains.

Leaving Salhouse, we descend for the next 2¾ miles, passing numerous lineside dwellings before slowing as we rumble past the diminutive Bridge Broad and over the River Bure where a large and varied assortment of river craft, boatyards, and riverside buildings greet the eye before we come to a stand in Hoveton and Wroxham station. Often special wagons for the conveyance of barley for the Scotch whisky industry are to be seen in the sidings.

A station said to have been intended for Wroxham was erected on the other side of the river in Hoveton (pronounced Hofften), using the signs prepared for Wroxham. In deference to the wishes of Hoveton Parish Council, which in 1986 defrayed the cost involved, British Rail renamed the station Hoveton and Wroxham, thus ending a long-standing injustice to Hoveton, the more developed and busier of the two villages.

30

The neighbouring parishes comprise the largest centre in Broadland, a flourishing, modern all-year-round shopping complex with restaurants and hotels, having grown tremendously since the days before the Second World War when Wroxham (Hoveton, to be correct), a rural boating centre, was reputed to possess the largest village store in the world. Based here is the Norfolk Broads Yacht Club, prominent in 'Cowes Week' as Wroxham Week is sometimes called. The mile-long Wroxham Broad is, however, not visible from the train.

Close behind the change of name came, unexpectedly, a remarkable change of use. Early in 1987 the station building was rejuvenated when part of it was transformed into an exclusive Italian restaurant with an interior resembling that of the famous Orient Express and embellished with the national colours of green, red and white.

On a single line now for the rest of the journey, we surmount the stiff rise out of Hoveton and note, bearing away on the left, a cutting through which ran a line connecting the village and small towns of central Norfolk. This line to County School (on the Wymondham–Dereham–Wells-next-the-Sea line) via Aylsham and Reepham closed to regular passenger trains as long ago as 1952, and more recently to freight traffic, but between 1976 and 1981 it was used by five excursion trains.

In February 1989, however, came the glad news of government approval for a narrow-gauge (15 in) steam railway as far as Aylsham, 8¾ miles from Hoveton, using the forsaken trackbed. Essentially a tourist attraction, though not without potential as a feeder for the British Rail network which the introduction of intermediate halts would further stimulate – one such has been agreed for Coltishall – the Bure Valley Railway hopes to be operative in 1990.

Continuing, mainly on the level, through typical Norfolk arable land, we draw up six minutes later at Worstead. In the twelfth century many wool-combers came over to England from Flanders and it was here at Worstead that the Flemings first settled and practised their craft. Their products came to be known as 'worsted' after the name of what in those days was a prosperous town, but is now merely a village. Held here in the summer each year is an attractive three-day festival, a magnet to thousands of people from and beyond the confines of Norfolk.

Conspicuous half a mile to the right is the fine parish church with its lofty embattled tower now bereft of its stately pinnacles which, added in 1844, were later damaged by lightning. The church, like that at North Walsham, our next stop, owes much to the weavers.

As we tackle the sharp climb out of Worstead we notice, on the left, in the woodlands of Westwick Park, a circular observation tower, not unlike a lighthouse, rising well above the treetops, ninety feet high and over 200 years old. Some years ago, alas, the tower was denuded of its attractive windowed octagonal summit apartment which commanded a superb vista of the north and east by a large extent of coastline.

Approaching North Walsham, a thriving market town with light industry, an attractive shopping precinct, and a market cross dating back to 1550, we pass on one side a large rose nursery, and on the other, parallel for some distance, a new road made on the bed of the former Midland & Great Northern Joint Railway (Great Yarmouth–Peterborough/Spalding–Bourne–Little Bytham) most of which was closed in 1959. The separate station in North Walsham is some 200 yards adjacent.

In North Walsham sidings, on the right, are rail-tankers used for the transport of condensate, a by-product in the recovery of natural gas from the North Sea, which is fed to the sidings from the Bacton gas installations a few miles away on the coast by means of a pipeline beneath the trackless bed of the North Walsham–Mundesley branch, closed in 1964.

Immediately on leaving North Walsham we rumble over the Norwich main road and behold on the left the fine sports ground of the Paston School where Nelson was a pupil for two years. Founded in 1606 by Sir William Paston, the grammar school was greatly enlarged and extended between the world wars. Since the autumn of 1984 it has been a co-educational Sixth Form College. In Grammar School Road, a short distance from the college entrance, is a cat pottery, where an interesting collection of railway memorabilia is also on view.

The college buildings can be glimpsed through the trees on the right, as can, and much more clearly, the ruined tower of the parish church, unusual in its shape and size and the second largest in Norfolk. Part of the tower fell down in 1724, another portion in 1835, and more the following year, when some of the remaining fragments, being in a dangerous state, were taken down. Further safety work on the tower was found necessary in 1939. Faulty construction and the elements account for the tower's unhappy history.

Moments later we cross another bridge spanning the trackless bed of the M & GN Railway, affectionately known as the 'muddle and get nowhere', whose trains at this point dived underneath on their way to North Norfolk's 'Little Crewe', the now defunct four-spoke hub of the joint railway situated at Melton Constable, seventeen miles westwards and near where the 'glorious Bure' has its source.

For about five miles in that direction to the outskirts of the market town of Aylsham the bed of the abandoned railway, unused for other purposes, today forms part of Weavers' Way, so called because of the importance of the weaving industry between the twelfth and eighteenth centuries. The disused line, as a local authority's lineside notice-board makes clear, is not a public right of way, but 'residents and visitors are permitted to use it at their own risk as a footpath and bridleway'. In a recess in Aylsham churchyard, incidentally, is the grave of Humphrey Repton (see also North Norfolk Railway).

So to Gunton, or rather the station so named. Gunton station – two miles and more east of Gunton Hall, an eighteenth century white brick mansion recently restored and converted into dwellings – was built at the expense of the fifth Lord Suffield, a big landowner and friend of King Edward VII. The spacious building still standing on the west-platform, once used by the landed gentry and royalty, is now a private house. Pot plants in the verandah and along the platform contribute to the traveller's pleasure during the train's brief pause here.

Near this isolated wayside station is an oasis of a public house. Named after the aforesaid nobleman who did so much to bring the iron road to Cromer and foster that resort's development, the inn successfully persuaded a sympathetic British Rail in 1985 to allow the last Sheringham–Norwich (limited stop) train to call at Gunton station for the benefit of Friday night drinkers, a concession appreciated and now operative every weekday night.

Much nearer to the station is Southrepps, its inhabitants housed in two clusters a mile apart. Conspicuous on the right when we draw out of the station is the 114-foot tower of the parish church, the glory of the village and a notable landmark.

Now comes a switchback for close on four miles: a stiff climb, then gradually down, then sharply up again to reach the Cromer–Holt Ridge, a legacy of the long departed glaciers.

Prior to September 1954, trains from Norwich bound for Cromer ran into Cromer High, a windswept terminal perched on an escarpment high above the town a mile away. For reasons of rationalisation and to the greater convenience of most travellers, the station of Great Eastern vintage, was closed and trains diverted to Cromer Beach, also a terminus, close to the sea front.

Norwich–Sheringham train descends Cromer Ridge (*Photo:* R. C. Vincent)

To reach this former M & GN station, we veer to the left a good half mile south of the now non-existent High station, then, at reduced speed, turn sharply west just short of the elegant underbridge at Roughton Road, the site of a new halt opened in 1985 and where the coastal or 'Poppy line' – so called because of the profusion of poppies in the area – to Overstrand, Sidestrand and Mundesley-on-Sea (part of the old Norfolk & Suffolk Joint Railway closed in 1953) diverged and descended to tunnel under the old High station goods yard. Roughton Road halt, three miles by rail from Cromer station, is idyllically situated amid woodlands and very convenient for those residents in the south-east district of Cromer, where, in recent years, housing estates have been developed.

From here we hasten along embankments and through wooded cuttings until the brakes go on as we prepare to make an inverted U-turn, from west to east, before descending slowly through a deep and winding cutting to draw up at one side or the other of the dual-faced platform of the now unstaffed terminus. Ahead of us we see the magnificent pinnacled tower of Cromer parish church rising to 160 feet, the highest in Norfolk and from which a light was nightly displayed on the seaward side before the erection of the 270-foot high lighthouse on the coastal hills to the east of the town.

It is on the section of line down to Cromer that we enjoy some fine views: our first glimpse of the sea, not forgetting the lighthouse, its beam visible twenty-three miles out to sea, and the cliffs and other areas dotted with holiday caravans and gaily coloured tents. The spindly mast visible in the south-west is the West Runton television transmitter, a booster for the Tacolneston television transmitter a few miles south of Norwich.

On the platform now is a substantial brick-built shelter of pleasing design, a replacement for a vandalised waiting-room demolished in 1986 along with toilets and the canopy embroidered with the initials of the Eastern & Midlands Railway which opened the station in 1887. The remaining station building, which is listed, is presently occupied by a firm of timber and builders' merchants.

At Cromer there is a short interval for reversal. The driver, confronted by the buffer stops, vacates his cab and strolls to the other end, ready to take us the remaining $3\frac{3}{4}$ miles. This, remnant of the once-proud M & GN Railway keeps within the national network the town of Sheringham, for many years the domicile of William Marriott, the monarch of the M & GN.

The wayfarer intent on exploring Cromer, the 'gem of the Norfolk coast', and perhaps scaling the lighthouse hills for the splendid views of the surrounding area – immortalised as 'Poppyland' by Clement Scott, the foremost dramatic critic of the late nineteenth century who devotedly frequented the district – will notice, to the left, wrought in the ironwork above the entrance of the former booking-hall the monogram of the old M & GN Railway which, in 1893, absorbed the earlier Eastern & Midlands Railway and, escaping the 1923 amalgamations, retained its separate identity until the unification of the railways in 1948.

Cromer, like North Walsham, is noted for a man who distinguished himself at sea, though in a very different rôle. Henry Blogg was for fifty-three years a lifeboatman and served thirty-eight of them as coxswain. In North Lodge Park a bronze bust of Blogg gazes out over the sea upon which during those many years close on 900 lives were saved by the Cromer lifeboat, its heroic history commemorated in a museum on the promenade below.

A spectacle particularly attractive to visitors is the launching of the lifeboat from a slipway at the end of the pier, the latter opened in 1901 by Lord Claud Hamilton, chairman of the Great Eastern Railway, who was so keen to develop rail traffic potential.

Next to the church is a museum illustrative of the Cromer fishing industry in the nineteenth century. An adaptation of five small fishermen's cottages, it is visited annually by many thousands.

Resuming our journey, we retrace our steps for half a mile as we head due west, the Norwich line curving away on our left. Gathering speed we hurry over a three-arch viaduct spanning a picturesque valley and East Runton village nestling below.

A short distance away on our left and roughly parallel is another viaduct, also of blue brick, one of five arches and considerably higher. This structure, open in

Cromer seafront

1906 and closed to traffic in 1963, carried a short line avoiding Cromer, and enabled such famous seasonal trains as the *Norfolk Coast Express* and the *Eastern Belle* – the latter an all-Pullman car excursion train resplendent in its two-tone livery of cream and umber, lined out in gold – to run direct between London's Liverpool Street station and Sheringham.

Darting from under a bridge, we hasten alongside the nine-hole (formerly eighteen-hole) West Runton golf-links fringed with hills covered in bracken and gorse, while on our right we gain a clear view of the sea and, in between, the Cromer to Sheringham road. Almost hidden in a dip is West Runton station, a wooden cabin-like structure in marked contrast to the well-appointed hotel astride the entrance to the links, little more than a stone's throw away.

The overbridge just beyond the concave platform carries the road to the so-called Roman Camp, a mile distant. This former beacon station which, at rather more than 300 feet above sea-level, is one of the highest points in Norfolk and affords panoramic views amid heather and bracken before a backcloth of varying shades of marine blue. This renowned beauty spot – its connection with the Roman occupation doubtful in the extreme – has been in the care of the National Trust since 1924. Teas and refreshments are obtainable here.

In a field on our left not far past the bridge are often to be seen horses and ponies of the Norfolk Shire Horse Centre and West Runton Riding Stables. As a working museum with a picnic area, souvenir shop and refreshment facilities, it is an extremely popular summer attraction.

Emerging from a wooded cutting, we notice on our right Beeston Regis church not far from the cliff. The church is expected to fall down onto the beach about the year 2129 because of the unremitting encroachments of the sea – a perennial problem along this coast of glacial cliffs formed of loose and incohesive material and further eroded by cliff drainage.

Then, into view on the left, come the tree-encircled ruins of Beeston Priory, a religious house dating back to the reign of King John in the thirteenth century. Tradition has it that a tunnel connects the two edifices separated by a mere half mile. In fact, a few years before the Second World War, some alterations being made in the adjacent Priory Farm led to the discovery of an entrance which was bricked up.

Also on the left, as the train slackens speed, can be seen Beeston Common, and, just beyond the coast road separating the two, Beeston Bog. The latter, golden in spring and summer with buttercups and gorse, is a naturalist's paradise where such plants as orchids and the elegant grass of Parnassus are to be found, while newts and frogs abound. The site has been designated by the Nature Conservancy Council as one of Special Scientific Interest.

At the same time, looming up on the right with its back to the cliff edge is Beeston Hill or Hump, though less prominent than of yore due to coastal erosion. A magnificent view of Sheringham and its hilly hinterland, and of the coastline, is the reward for those prepared to make the steep ascent to the top.

Spreading out before us now, on both sides of an embankment, is Sheringham, and after crossing a couple of bridges and passing on our left and red brick Roman Catholic Church of St Joseph designed by Sir Giles Gilbert Scott, we come gently to a halt at a short wooden asphalted platform which today serves as the Sheringham railhead, thirty and a half miles from Norwich.

A far cry, this, from the halcyon days when in 1906 the Great Eastern Railway, nicknamed 'Swedey' because of its considerable traffic in the Swedish turnip, gained the right to run to Sheringham, which for some years thereafter enjoyed distinction and luxury of two station-masters, each in his separate office on the same platform supervising the arrival and departure of his company's trains.

NORTH NORFOLK RAILWAY

by Wallace Boyles

```
                                    Ⓣtb;B;Bks; LG;taxi
    HOLT                            SHERINGHAM
    ▢━━━━━━━━━━━━━▢━━━━━━━━━━━━━▢ ●  - - - -
                  WEYBOURNE                  Sheringham BR
                  Bks-dks;LG                 Ⓣt S Sr
```

Alighting from the British Rail train at Sheringham we see just ahead across the busy Station Road, which once had a level crossing and signal-box, the original station, the buildings on the north platform still in being and now the headquarters of the North Norfolk Railway. The line from Melton Constable to Sheringham, 11¼ miles, was closed in 1964, and part of it was subsequently bought for re-opening as a preserved line.

The car-park adjacent to the station was an extensive goods yard and from here, for some years before and after the Second World War, flints gathered from the beach were dispatched to Stoke-on-Trent for use in the manufacture of pottery. Now, on Saturdays, against a background of stored locomotives and passenger rolling-stock, part of the yard is the scene of a market of some sixty stalls.

In 1976, the North Norfolk Railway began to operate under its own Light Railway Transfer Order, having the previous year run some summer weekend passenger trains with British Rail's agreement. From Sheringham, between Easter and the end of September, and at certain other times – such as the popular Santa Specials run at Christmas – the NNR has operated a steam and diesel service, initially to Weybourne, 2¾ miles distant.

The line has since been steadily restored and extended beyond Weybourne to a halt at Kelling Heath Park, giving access to a caravan site and the newly-opened Kelling Heath Nature Trail and, finally, to a point in High Kelling adjacent to Kelling Hospital and within a stone's throw of Holt parish boundary. Unfortunately, this is more than a mile from Holt town due to the demolition at this point of an awkward humpback bridge which carried the main road over the abandoned branch line and also the subsequent utilisation westwards of some of that line for a bypass.

The reinstated line has now a length of 5¼ miles and will this year (1989) be fully operative. For the western extremity on the outskirts of Holt, a platform, preparatory to the building of a station, has been provided and designated as Holt. A subsequent change of name to High Kelling and Holt is envisaged.

A timetable for the North Norfolk Railway, also indicating the dates on which it operates, is obtainable from Sheringham station (telephone 822045).

Trains steam slowly out, past the golf-links on the right with Sheringham's new tropical paradise (The Splash) on the left, and climb steadily through undulating fields with good views of the wooded hills to the south and the sea to the north. To the left, shortly before the bridge which carries the line over the coast road is Sheringham Hall, regarded as the masterpiece of the eighteenth-century architect and landscape designer, Humphrey Repton, himself an East Anglian born at Bury St Edmunds.

In 1986, Sheringham Hall was acquired by the National Trust which has opened to the public the superb estate of 770 acres of woodlands, gardens and parkland, in summer gorgeous with rhododendrons and azaleas, and a mile of coastline designated as an area of Special Scientific Interest. Newly erected on high ground in the park is a thirty-four-foot tall gazebo. Officially opened and greatly admired

Class J15 0-6-0 no. 7564 arrives at Weybourne station (*Photo:* Brian Fisher)

Restored diesel railbus no. E79960 (with no. 79963 coupled behind) at Weybourne station
(*Photo:* Brian Fisher)

by Prince Charles in 1988, it affords a breathtaking view of the countryside and 'a very special coastline', as the Prince described it. Provision of a halt to afford convenient access to the park is under consideration.

Weybourne station, the starting point for the nature trail and where the workshops are located, is situated in a sylvan setting roughly a mile inland from the coastal village. Close to the shore is deep water, and it is here that the Angles, and later the Danes, are believed to have made their landings, hence the ancient local rhyme:

> 'He who would old England win,
> Must at Weybourne Hope begin.'

The establishment at Weybourne in 1935 of an anti-aircraft practice camp brought much additional traffic to the station, which continued until the camp was abandoned fourteen years after the war ended. A year or two before the war, a group of senior German officers came to Weybourne to watch a demonstration of gunnery, and Churchill visited it twice during the war. The Muckleburgh Collection, a large museum of privately-owned and restored military vehicles from the last war is now on the site and open to the public.

This sleepy village has also played a vital role in international communications: in 1950, a submarine cable was laid from here to Esbjerg by a Danish company, who closed the Weybourne telegraph repeater station in 1987.

In recent years the Sheringham–Weybourne stretch of line has figured in a number of television productions, among them *Dad's Army, Hi-di-Hi, 'Allo 'Allo, Swallows and Amazons, Fall of Eagles,* D. H. Lawrence's famous novel *Sons and Lovers,* and the late Sir John Betjeman's programme *A Passion for Churches,* in the filming of which the Poet Laureate travelled in a special train.

The steep mile-long rise (1 in 80) immediately before Weybourne continues for another mile beyond the station. Through cuttings and along embankments made colourful with bluebells and primroses, or bracken and heather, according to the time of year, the line winds to scale the Ridge at Kelling Heath. In the vicinity, restored and re-opened, is Kelling Aviaries, an area of seven acres devoted to exotic birds and other animals, including a bird hospital.

Towards Holt the ground levels out. From the end of the line to the market town of Holt – Georgian in appearance following a disastrous fire in 1708 which destroyed most of the town – is a walk taking the sightseer past Gresham's School (1555) where three twentieth-century figures were educated: the poet and dramatist W. H. Auden, the Lowestoft-born composer Benjamin Britten, who was ennobled shortly before his death, and Lord Reith of the BBC.

For those disposed to explore Sheringham, having perhaps returned from a trip on the preserved railway and visited the excellent picture gallery in Holt which no lover of art should miss, there is Franklin (Hook's) Hill, about 200 feet in height where one can enjoy views comparable with those from Beeston Hill. And rather more than a mile south of the station is Pretty Corner, another of Norfolk's highest points, a beauty spot set in a heathery hinterland.

Unlike Cromer, Sheringham has not the advantage of a pier, and its lifeboat, housed at the end of the west promenade at right angles to the sea is launched by means of a turntable. To Sheringham belongs the proud distinction of having saved more airmen's lives during the Second World War than any other lifeboat station in Great Britain. And crabs landed at Sheringham are the equal of Cromer crabs, the latter traditionally famous because of the alliteration!

Outside the station, its former parcels office now an attractive buffet and souvenir shop, is a putting-green laid out with flower-beds and seats. In the town centre, where the stocks once stood, is a quaint clock tower and shelter. The tower was built in 1862 and there was a reservoir where women fetched water and horses drank from a trough. The clock was erected in 1901 as a citizen's 'Easter offering'. Some thirty or more years ago the reservoir was converted into a diminutive windowed shelter.

The North Norfolk Railway is a useful point of departure for ramblers. Westwards, for example, one can follow the cliff and golf-links almost into the village of Weybourne and then, turning inland along a track to strike the coast road by the inhabited five-storey tower windmill, make for the station and journey back to Sheringham by train.

WHERRY LINE
by Trevor Garrod

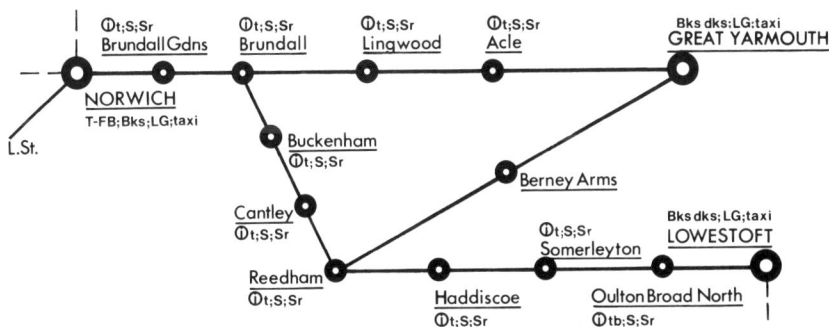

Ⓘt;S;Sr   Ⓘt;S;Sr   Ⓘt;S;Sr   Ⓘt;S;Sr   Bks dks;LG;taxi
BrundallGdns   Brundall   Lingwood   Acle   GREAT YARMOUTH

NORWICH
T-FB;Bks;LG;taxi

L.St.

Buckenham
Ⓘt;S;Sr

Berney Arms

Cantley
Ⓘt;S;Sr

Bks dks;LG;taxi
LOWESTOFT

Ⓘt;S;Sr
Somerleyton

Reedham
Ⓘt;S;Sr

Haddiscoe
Ⓘt;S;Sr

Oulton Broad North
Ⓘtb;S;Sr

The wherry was a wooden barge whose large sail moved slowly across the flat east Norfolk landscape as it bore its cargoes along the winding Waveney, Yare, and Bure, down the smaller rivers and across the main Broads. Trading wherries are long since gone, and apart from a very few cargo vessels to Norwich, the rivers and lakes are now the preserve of cruisers, yachts, and other pleasure craft.

Memories of the old vessels were revived by British Rail in 1974 when they christened the 'Wherry line': the group of lines between Norwich, Great Yarmouth and Lowestoft, over which diesel railcars provide a fast and frequent service – never far from water, serving several riverside communities en route.

On leaving Norwich, Wherry Line trains are soon speeding along the left bank of the Yare, an old branch of which skirts Thorpe village, backed by luxuriant rising woodland, just to the north. Five miles along the line is Brundall, a growing commuter village with a station and also a halt (Brundall Gardens) built in 1924. The train runs through woodland with glints of water on either side, past boatyards, a large pub and, a short walk from the station, the river Yare among beds of reed, alder, and willow. In summer, you can enjoy a leisurely trip by pleasure boat between Foundry Bridge (by entrance to Norwich station) and Brundall.

A pleasant run through alders and willows, with Strumpshaw Fen Bird Reserve on the right, brings us to the isolated station of Buckenham, 7¾ miles from Norwich, with an octagonal church tower peering over rising land to the left. Now the Yare Valley marshes open out, the river winding between dikes to the south of us, interrupted only by Cantley dominated by the impressive silos of its sugar-beet factory, from which dense white smoke billows during the autumn.

Reedham Ferry – the only crossing for road vehicles between Norwich and

Train passing Berney Arms Mill (*Photo:* R. C. Vincent)

Great Yarmouth – can be seen to the south as we pull into the station serving the large riverside village. At Reedham, Great Yarmouth trains take a single track straight across the marshes, sometimes pausing on the way at the other station in the parish of Reedham – Berney Arms.

Berney Arms is unique – a riverside pub, one or two isolated farms, and a massive windmill in the middle of flat pastureland, with no road access but instead, a tiny windswept platform. Once a week, a postman comes out by train from Great Yarmouth to deliver mail. Some trains stop only when required. Berney Arms Mill is open from April to the end of September.

In the mid-1980s, this line was threatened with closure, owing to the relatively high cost of replacing ageing track and sleepers; but an alliance of thirteen local authorities and voluntary bodies (including the Railway Development Society) successfully negotiated a contract with British Rail to pay half the cost of refurbishment over a five-year period. For the signing of the contract in May 1987, the General Manager's saloon was filled with representatives of the thirteen contributing bodies, and pulled out on to the marshes.

Soon the train rounds the northern edge of Breydon Water with its varied wildlife. On rising ground to the south can be seen the low stone walls of Burgh Castle – the Roman fort of Garianonum built to defend what was then a great estuary from Saxon marauders.

Some twenty and a half miles from Norwich, the train runs past sidings and enters the curving platforms of Vauxhall Station – the only survivor of Great Yarmouth's three stations, damaged in the Second World War and largely rebuilt in 1960. Freight facilities were withdrawn from the adjacent yard in 1984; while previously in 1976 the rail line which crossed the River Bure, at the station approach, and gave access to the South Quay, was also closed. The view across the water is now dominated by the distinctive bypass bridge, opened in 1986; while next to the station an Asda superstore has been built on former freight sidings.

Great Yarmouth remains a busy port, but all freight must currently go by road. Most visitors to the town are likely to head across the River Bure to find themselves within a few minutes of the extensive pedestrianised market-place with the stately

40

Church of St Nicholas at one end and the Market Gates Shopping Centre at the other. The museums and remains of medieval walls are a less well-known aspect of this town which most people will know as one of the leading resorts of the east coast. With neighbouring Gorleston it boasts six miles of sandy beaches, and the central Golden Mile, with the greatest concentration of holiday attractions, is some twenty minutes' walk from the station.

The Lowestoft trains rattle over Reedham Swing Bridge (with good views of the waterfront), then bear left to run alongside the New Cut, a $2\frac{1}{2}$ mile canal cut straight as a die from the Yare to the Waveney in 1833, to reach Norwich by way of Lowestoft rather than Great Yarmouth. The two coastal towns have long been rivals.

In fact, the Norwich–Lowestoft Navigation had a brief heyday – partly because the Great Yarmouth Port and Haven Commissioners undertook works to improve their own passage to Norwich; and partly because of the building of this railway in 1847. The New Cut is nowadays used purely by pleasure craft.

Just before Haddiscoe, the train passes under a concrete road bridge built across the line and the New Cut in 1960. Haddiscoe station is over a mile and a half from the village of that name, but rather closer to St Olaves, a hamlet on the opposite bank of the Waveney, set among trees. Legend has it that the Viking Olaf (Olave) and his longboat haunt the river in these parts. There is a pleasant riverside pub in St Olaves and a ruined priory (entry free). A mile farther east is Fritton with a church of Saxon origin and a long serpentine lake in woodland, with a country park open to the public in summer.

Indeed, there is much of interest in Lothingland, this northern tip of Suffolk (some of whose parishes were transferred to Norfolk in 1974) – the churches of Ashby and Lound, Somerleyton Hall and Gardens, Burgh Castle, and Blundeston with its Dickensian associations. It is good cycling country, and Haddiscoe or Somerleyton stations are ideal railheads from which to explore it.

The train passes the earthworks of the former Beccles – Great Yarmouth line at Haddiscoe (once a two-level interchange) and follows the curves of the Waveney to Somerleyton, a picturesque station designed to please the lord of the manor. The railway gives a better view of the restored Herringfleet Mill than any road can. These marshes were once peppered with such pumping mills. The Wherry Line is now in Suffolk and soon gives views of Oulton Church, with its unusual central tower, on rising land to the left; while opposite, on the Norfolk side of the Waveney, is the Church of Burgh St Peter, with its curious five-stage bell tower, nestling in trees on the river bank.

A quick run through leafy suburbs brings our train to Oulton Broad North, conveniently situated for the nearby lake with its park, swimming pool, and other attractions, including bank holiday fêtes and speedboat-racing in summer. We then follow the same route as the East Suffolk line trains into Lowestoft, where we can smell the salt air as we alight at the station, the most easterly on British Rail. A mere stone's throw away is the harbour with its trawlers, and two minutes' walk over the bascule bridge is the sandy beach. Outside the station, a statue, *The Call of the Sea*, actually points the way along the town's pedestrianised main shopping street, towards the rival resort of Great Yarmouth.

An alternative rail route to Great Yarmouth leaves the main line at Brundall and heads for Lingwood – which the sailing wherries never reached. Wherry Line trains serve this growing commuter village on the direct Brundall–Great Yarmouth line opened in 1883, and continue through undulating wheat fields dotted with typical Norfolk round-towered churches to Acle – a large village with a well-known cattle market – before striking out across the marshes, parallel to the A47 to join the older route from Reedham on the shores of Breydon Water.

EAST SUFFOLK LINE

by Louis Hipperson

LG taxi — T-FB:Bks — IPSWICH · Café(summer) Ⓣtb S Sr G Woodbridge · Ⓣt S Sr Wickham Market · Ⓣtb S Sr taxi Darsham · Ⓣtb S Sr Brampton · Ⓣtb S Sr Oulton Broad South

Westerfield Ⓣtb S Sr · Melton Ⓣt Sr taxi · Saxmundham Ⓣtb S Sr LG Restaurant (MX) · Halesworth Ⓣtb S Sr · Beccles Ⓣt S Sr · LOWESTOFT Bks-dks LG taxi

This line (opened throughout in 1859) runs from Ipswich, Suffolk's county town, to Lowestoft, in the north-east of the county and its second town in size. Much of the seaward side of Suffolk is served, including several small towns of considerable historic and other interest.

Work costing at least £1,600,000 was carried out on the line between 1982 and 1985 to reduce running and maintenance costs. For most of the route, signalling has been radically altered. Between Westerfield station and Oulton Broad South station all signal boxes, except one, were removed. The sole remaining one, at Saxmundham station, acts as a computerised control centre and communicates with train drivers by means of radio. Formerly double track throughout, much of the line has been singled. Gates to public level crossings have been replaced by flashing lights and sirens which, operated by the train passing over track circuits, warn road traffic to stop. In some cases half or full barriers act as additional protection.

From Ipswich to Beccles, on the Norfolk border, the line forms an approximate demarcation between two of Suffolk's geographical regions. Between the railway and the coast are the Sandlings, once almost completely covered with heaths, and grazed by large flocks of sheep. The heaths are now much diminished and the sheep have vanished. The light soil is increasingly being brought under the plough or afforested. West of the railway lies so-called High Suffolk, a low plateau, from which many rivers and streams flow into the North Sea; the railway, therefore, crosses a large number of valleys of varying character. As no viaducts or high embankments were built to carry the line, it has, by railway standards, a surprising number of quite steep gradients. This may seem strange to those who imagine that all East Anglia is flat as a pancake. The physical geography, together with the many small woods and isolated trees still existing in the neighbourhood of the line, produces scenery that, while not spectacular, is very pleasant.

The directions 'right' and 'left' in the following description of a journey along the line are based on the assumption that the reader is seated facing towards the front of the train. Figures in parenthesis after the name of a station indicate its mileage from Ipswich.

Within a mile of leaving Ipswich, the train diverges from the main Norwich line at East Suffolk Junction. The route as far as Westerfield (3½), the first station, is described in the section Ipswich–Felixstowe. Beyond Westerfield, the train, now travelling almost due east, passes through a succession of cuttings above the River Fynn (or Finn), a little to the north. An automated, open level crossing marks the site of Bealings station (7¼), whose passenger service was withdrawn in 1956. Two minutes later we cross the Fynn and almost at once note on the right Martlesham Creek (an inlet of the River Deben) into which the Fynn flows. Next come extensive nurseries on each side.

The line curves north-east to reveal a general view of the town of Woodbridge on the left. Opposite, close at hand, is the estuary of the Deben, backed by rising, partly wooded, countryside. Between rail and river is a delightful promenade with model yacht pond and bandstand. We see a large number of yachts, cruisers and other pleasure craft. Woodbridge Station (10¼) is a stone's throw from the water's edge. Nearby are an eighteenth-century tide-mill (open to visitors), thought to be the last now working in Britain, and a modern swimming-pool.

Apart from its aquatic interest, Woodbridge is one of the most attractive towns in Suffolk. It has the fine fifteenth-century parish church of St Mary, a small museum, many beautiful buildings, a public school, an abundance of hotels, pubs and eating-places, and an excellent range of shops. Limited tourist information is available in the public library, New Street, or St Mary's Information Centre, Market Hill.

On high ground on the other side of the Deben and within one mile of Woodbridge station (but much longer by road), is one of the most important archaeological sites in Europe. This is Sutton Hoo, best known for its seventh-century ship burial discovered in 1939. The vessel is now thought by most archaeologists to have served as the tomb of an East Anglian king of the Wuffinga dynasty, probably Redwald. Chemical analysis of the soil has shown traces of phosphate, a result of disintegrating bones. The priceless treasures found in the ship are in the British Museum, although replicas exist in Ipswich Museum and a permanent Sutton Hoo exhibition is in Woodbridge Museum. At weekends and on bank holiday Mondays during the summer, Sutton Hoo is open to the public, but for guided tours only. Participants are taken across the river by a special ferry service, times being shown on a notice-board at the quayside.

The bus station is only a few minutes' walk from the railway station. On leaving the station exit, immediately bear right towards a delightful restaurant, part of a block that includes the Riverside Theatre and cinema. Pass in front of the restaurant into Quayside and continue 250 yards to finger-post marked 'car-park' then left into the Turban Centre, a complex that includes the bus station. Buses run to Framlingham, another attractive town, with a ruined twelfth-century castle (mainly curtain walls and towers), a Late Perpendicular church (notable

River Deben at Woodbridge

tombs, some with effigies) and Framlingham College, the Suffolk county memorial to the Prince Consort; to Wickham Market, a quiet little town, its most noticeable feature the lofty spire of its church; and to the village of Orford (essential to obtain bus times in advance), a quaint, decayed pocket borough close to the coast – see the partly ruined church and Norman polygonal castle keep (the first of its shape in England) and eat locally-bred oysters.

Our train continues past Melton, a suburb of Woodbridge. Melton Station ($11\frac{1}{2}$) had its passenger service restored from 3 September 1984, after being without one since 1955. Woodbridge–Orford buses pass the station.

We keep to the Deben Valley after Melton, but the river is now much reduced in width and ceases to be navigable. Within a distance of three miles, we cross the river as many times.

Wickham Market station ($15\frac{3}{4}$) is actually in the village of Campsea Ashe (or Campsey Ash), two miles from the town after which it is named. Public transport linking station and town is practically nil. From this station, branch line passenger trains ran to Framlingham until 1952, but the rails have been lifted, leaving few vestiges of the route.

Just beyond the station, on the right, is a close view of the village church, its tower crowned by a spirelet. Soon we go through a double line of electricity pylons, leading to the nuclear power station at Sizewell on the coast, and descend to follow for a short distance the valley of a tributary of the River Alde. Crossing the main river, we can look over the marshes on the right to the distant Snape Maltings, now of concert fame but served until 1960 by a freight-only branch, traces of which are difficult to discern.

Three miles farther on, we drop down to the compact little town of Saxmundham, nestling in the valley of the Fromus, another tributary of the Alde. The station ($22\frac{1}{2}$) is the railhead for Leiston and Aldeburgh, both larger than Saxmundham, and the twentieth-century planned village of Thorpeness. Buses run from Saxmundham to all three places, although the service to Thorpeness is sparse. The

Snape Maltings

June 1983, the 14.58 Ipswich–Lowestoft train pauses at Saxmundham station while passengers await the arrival of the 14.50 Lowestoft–Ipswich (*Photo:* Howard Quayle)

bus station, in High Street, next to the modern post office and telephone exchange, is reached on foot in five minutes from the railway station by descending to the T-junction and turning left.

Leiston was only a village until the nineteenth-century development of its ironworks, founded in 1778 but closed down completely in 1980. Among its remaining buildings is the Long Shop, a regional industrial museum. The local economy now depends to a large extent on the nuclear power stations at Sizewell, a coastal hamlet within the parish of Leiston. Aldeburgh, a very pleasant seaside resort completely free of garish amusements, is internationally famous for its annual musical festival, held every June and linked with the late Benjamin Britten, the Lowestoft-born composer. Among other notables connected with Aldeburgh was the poet George Crabbe, born here in 1754. The cinema, in High Street, provides accommodation for a tourist information centre from April to September.

A short climb from Saxmundham brings us to the junction with the single-track branch line (right) used for taking waste from the nuclear power station at Sizewell. Until 1966, this line carried a passenger service to Leiston, Thorpeness and Aldeburgh, but now ends a little short of Sizewell.

The next station, Darsham ($26\frac{3}{4}$), entered by a level crossing over the main London to Great Yarmouth road, is some way from Darsham village and $1\frac{1}{2}$ miles from the much larger village of Yoxford on the Minsmere River (or Yox) and called 'the garden of Suffolk'. The walker or cyclist who alights at Darsham, as at other stations on the line, can visit the Suffolk Heritage Coast, with its long-distance footpath. In addition, Darsham is the most convenient station for those wishing to explore the varied countryside surrounding the villages of Westleton and Dunwich, the latter probably the outstanding example in Britain of a large historic town and seaport almost completely lost through cliff erosion. A little to the south of Dunwich is the renowned bird sanctuary of Minsmere.

Having descended to Darsham, we rise again to go through a series of cuttings

45

parallel to the road through the village of Bramfield (right), where it is sometimes possible to catch a brief sight of the church's detached round tower. As soon as we clear the cuttings, we cross the road on the level and in a few seconds we can see it curving away to the left into the town of Halesworth, the modern development of which is visible – it has doubled in size since the Second World War. The train now goes down one of the steepest gradients on the line into the valley of the River Blyth. About a mile away, half-right, the restored wooden post-mill, painted white, at Holton takes the eye.

The train enters Halesworth Station (32) over a bridge above the Southwold road. Between 1879 and 1929, trains ran between these towns along a single-track, narrow-gauge railway. But all traces of the separate Southwold railway station that was immediately to the right of Halesworth station, have disappeared under recent housing development.

The old part of Halesworth, with its narrow winding streets, repays exploration. It contains the large parish church of St Mary with double aisles on each side, and many other interesting buildings.

Southwold, nine miles east of Halesworth, is a seaside town noted for its unspoilt character (reminiscent of more leisurely days), magnificent Perpendicular church (dedicated to St Edmund, patron of East Anglia), museum, lighthouse and breezy common. A tourist information centre is open in the Town Hall, Market Place, from early June to late August.

Nine miles north of Halesworth is Bungay, with yet another castle, two medieval churches, a butter cross, a very large common in a loop of the River Waveney, and Richard Clay plc, Britain's biggest book printers.

It is possible to travel by bus between Halesworth and both Southwold and Bungay (except to the latter on Sunday). The bus-stops are fairly close to the railway station. For Southwold, leave the station on the down side, turning left downhill as soon as the road is reached. At the T-junction turn right into Quay Street and wait outside the United Reformed Church, a little way along on the right. To catch a bus for Bungay, again leave the station on the down side, but follow a footpath alongside the railway. On arrival at Norwich Road, you will find the bus-stop on the opposite side, a few yards away to the right and over the bridge. Those who wish to explore Halesworth may find it more convenient to catch a bus from the bus stand at Steeple End, adjoining the far side of the churchyard.

From Halesworth station, the train makes a long ascent, passing, at a level crossing within the first half mile, the site of the terminal station of the Halesworth, Beccles and Haddiscoe Railway (opened 1854), the nucleus of the East Suffolk line. Over a mile from the present Halesworth station, we pass under a road bridge and then the gradient eases.

The train descends to Brampton station (36), well over two miles from the main part of the village of that name, but very soon and much nearer on the left, we see the small village of Redisham. The late Adrian Bell, the renowned writer on country matters, lived for some years in its Old Vicarage.

Three miles beyond Brampton, after a switchback ride, we again reach the top of a long descent (Beccles Bank) to reach within two or three minutes the outskirts of the market and manufacturing town of Beccles. Our downhill course extends almost to Beccles station (40½), formerly by far the most important and largest intermediate one on the line and now but the merest shadow of its pre-Beeching days. Up to 1959, it was a junction. In that year the Beccles–Great Yarmouth (Southtown) section of the East Suffolk line was closed to passengers. The line from Beccles via Bungay to Tivetshall (on the main Ipswich–Norwich line) had been similarly closed in 1953. Both lines have now been lifted, although infrequent buses run on weekdays from Beccles to Great Yarmouth and Bungay. The bus station, in Old Market, is under ten minutes' walk from the railway station. Follow Station Road towards the town centre (signed) and, at the next crossroads *after* the traffic lights, turn right into Smallgate, continuing to the far end of that street. A few Bungay buses start from the railway station.

Beccles Parish Church of St Michael is of noble proportions. It has a massive stone-faced, detached tower (visible from the train) and a beautifully carved stone south porch. The town is a well-known Broadland centre, being situated on the River Waveney, here a county boundary, the opposite bank being in Norfolk. From the station, we can see (left) the extensive works of the eminent printers William Clowes Ltd, noted for reference works and other books of high quality. A tourist information centre is open at the town quay from Easter to the end of September.

Just beyond the station platforms, watch out for the former small engine-shed (left). The line is now bearing gradually to the east. The level crossing over the Beccles bypass indicates the site of the junction with the Great Yarmouth line, whose course can be traced bearing slightly left. We traverse several miles of marshes, but the scenery is not monotonous owing to the woods on either side. At one point, the train runs for about a mile close to the main Beccles–Lowestoft road – and overtakes all traffic!

On the left lies Carlton Marshes nature reserve, with its newly-built Visitor Centre, shortly before we draw into Oulton Broad South station (46¾). The driver speaks for the last time on his radio to Saxmundham control, relinquishes the electronic token and presently we rattle across the swing bridge over Lake Lothing, a sheet of water that stretches away to the right to reach Lowestoft harbour. To our left we can see another expanse of water, Oulton Broad, usually a hive of activity. A few hundred yards farther on, we pass the ends of the platforms at Oulton Broad North station (left) and join the Norwich–Lowestoft route to finish our journey at Lowestoft station (49).

(*Note:* At all stations on the East Suffolk line, the official British Rail timetable is supplemented by a separate board of useful information, including local bus timetables, maintained by the East Suffolk Travellers' Association.)

Oulton Broad

IPSWICH–FELIXSTOWE

by Howard Quayle

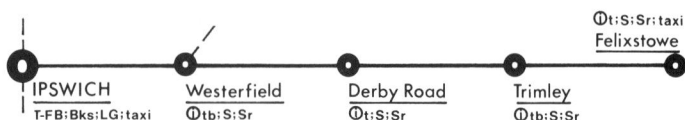

Ⓣt:S:Sr:taxi
Felixstowe

IPSWICH   Westerfield   Derby Road   Trimley
T-FB:Bks:LG:taxi   Ⓣtb:S:Sr   Ⓣt:S:Sr   Ⓣtb:S:Sr

This line remains the only 'classical' East Anglian branch never to have been proposed for closure, and the reasons why are not hard to see – healthy all-year-round commuter traffic, enhanced by holiday-makers during the summer, and still-expanding base of Freightliner traffic from the port of Felixstowe.

The line's route out of Ipswich is unusual, since it virtually doubles back on itself to reach the town's eastern suburbs, 1½ miles away as the crow flies, but six miles distant for the rail traveller! This is because Felixstowe trains use the East Suffolk line as far as Westerfield, reached after a steep climb of 1 in 90/150 across high embankments and through deep cuttings. Westerfield station (3½ miles from Ipswich) is a typical rural halt, with its 'bus-stop' shelters, although, on the right, wooden buildings erected in 1877 by the Felixstowe Railway & Pier Co. still survive. These shabby relics may yet be restored, thanks to their recent purchase by a private owner.

With the picturesque village of Westerfield on the left, the train runs past the signalbox and curves southwards along a single line, climbing at 1 in 85. Our diesel multiple unit has been running through the countryside since before Westerfield and the unwary find it strange to plunge back once more into suburban Ipswich, the line having completed its arc from Ipswich station.

Once across the Spring Road viaduct – the line's major engineering work with a fine but fleeting view of the town to the right – the train enters the loop at Derby Road station (six miles from Ipswich) where the sidings still generate some freight traffic.

The single line now leaves Ipswich for the second time, and with the Suffolk Showground on the left, plunges into the forest area around the exclusive village of Nacton; here a single-span bridge, completed in 1982, carries the branch over its major competitor, the dual carriageway A45. Beyond lie the remains of Orwell station, closed in 1959 when diesel trains were introduced and services accelerated.

Emerging from the Scottish-type scenery of the pine forest, the train now runs along virtually dead-level track. The outlines of villages are prominent in the flat landscape, as are the tall buildings of the British Telecom Research Centre, away to the east at Martlesham. To the west, however, come views of coastal Suffolk, glimpses of the Orwell estuary being followed by vistas of the modern port of Felixstowe.

Running into Trimley station (fourteen miles from Ipswich), where tokens are exchanged for the last time, our train gives a view of Felixstowe Docks close at hand, contrasting with the medieval town of Harwich on the other side of the Stour. Particularly dominant are St Nicholas Church and the pagoda-inspired lighthouse, one of the earliest in Britain. From Trimley station, a 1½-mile long branch, opened on 2 March 1987, drops away due south to serve the port's north Freightliner terminal, opened four years earlier. The opening ceremonies included the naming of class 47 locomotive 47251 as *The Port of Felixstowe*.

Speed is now down to 20 mph as the line curves into the cutting at Felixstowe Beach Junction, the freight-only dock line diverging to the right, and a minute

Felixstowe Town station – the 1898 terminus building, now renamed Great Eastern Square, is part of a shopping complex (*Photo:* Russell Whipps)

later the train comes to a halt in the single-platformed Felixstowe station ($5\frac{1}{2}$ miles from Ipswich.)

The main part of the town's station – built in 1898 during its late Victorian heyday as a fashionable resort – has been converted into a shopping centre, called Great Eastern Square. Passengers can walk through this tastefully restored complex and straight down Hamilton Road – a pleasant thoroughfare with some shops still retaining their Victorian facades – to the sea front.

Although the latter may have more attraction for many, the town itself, which grew up in the late nineteenth century at the top of the hill above the promenade, is well worth a close look. Because of its rapid growth between 1881 and 1891, the architectural style displays a homogeneity not often found elsewhere, although the observant visitor may notice, intermingled with solid Victorian red brick, the flamboyant designs of T. W. Cotman, a noted local architect. His crowning triumph was undoubtedly the neo-Jacobean Felix Hotel in Cobbold Road, dating from 1903, now converted into luxury flats.

The seafront at the foot of the low cliffs has all the attractions of larger resorts: pier, funfair, cafés and restaurants, and invigorating sea breezes. Safe beaches and the sight of ships in the busy shipping lanes offshore make Felixstowe a very pleasant place in which to spend a few hours. Since 1985, a new leisure centre incorporating an excellent swimming-pool and indoor bowling-green have enhanced the amenities.

Finally, ramblers and nature-lovers may note that Felixstowe is the southern terminus of the fifty-mile Suffolk Coastal Path to Lowestoft, for which Suffolk County Council has produced an attractive brochure. A ferry operates as required across the Deben estuary at the northern end of the town; while at the southern end there is a two-hourly ferry service in summer to Harwich, and less frequent crossings in winter.

MANNINGTREE–HARWICH

by John Hull

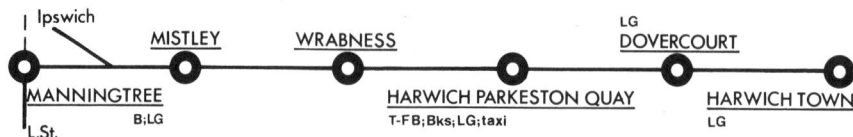

Opened in 1854, the 11¼-mile line from Manningtree to Harwich is really two completely different railways: on the one hand it is a fairly typical branch line, with trains departing from a bay platform at a junction station and proceeding to call at a succession of small stations until it reaches a terminus in a moderately sized coastal town. On the other hand, it is a busy double-track main line carrying heavy freight and passenger traffic from all over the country to one of its major ports.

The best way to see the line's two faces is to board one of the electric multiple units that provide at least an hourly service from Manningtree, mostly working through from London. From this station, whose buffet has a large number of real ales on sale, the train immediately curves away from the main line, heading eastwards to climb out of, but never leave, the valley of the River Stour. The train window affords magnificent views across the water to the Suffolk side a mile or so away.

Passing through Manningtree town in a steeply graded cutting, out train reaches open countryside just before its first stop at Mistley, probably the best remaining example of a wayside station in East Anglia. It is staffed, with proper booking-office and waiting-room, and still has freight sidings. The station is surrounded by maltings, some traditional and one very modern, while at the bottom of the steep slope behind them is a small quay.

From Mistley, the train soon emerges onto a high embankment, with views northwards to the Royal Hospital School at Holbrook, whose slender tower dominates the Suffolk bank of the estuary. Speed rises as the remains of Bradfield station (closed in 1956) are passed, followed quickly by the remnants of Priory Halt, a platform built to serve the Royal Naval Mine Depot, now closed. Wrabness soon comes into view, another delightful station serving an isolated village. From here it is only a twenty-minute walk to a very pleasant river beach on the banks of the Stour.

For the next two miles, the train runs through woodland, mostly chestnut which until recently was used commercially for fencing. In the autumn the varying colours make a most impressive sight, particularly to the north with the river as a backdrop. Then suddenly, the real reason for the line's present existence comes into view, as the train drops from the higher valley side and turns on to the marshes. Originally, it would have continued in a straight line, but when the Great Eastern Railway came into conflict with Harwich Borough in the 1870s, it decided to build a new port on the marshy Ray Island, just outside the Corporation's boundary. Hence the creation of Parkeston Quay, opened in 1883 and named after the then Chairman of the company.

The port itself has been totally rebuilt over the past two decades to cater for modern traffic. It remains very busy, even though road traffic now intrudes on what was once solely a rail port – much to the annoyance of local residents.

Running through the freight yards, we can see the large passenger ferries to the north before our train runs into one of the three long platforms of Parkeston

Quay station. The original red-brick nineteenth-century building is still there, but modern customs halls and other facilities have been built on to it, and boat passengers can now walk from train to ferry completely under cover.

Boat-trains from London terminate at Parkeston Quay, as do the Sprinter services from the Midlands and the north-west; but our local train continues along a single track, swinging back across the marshes towards the original route, passing the container terminal on the left and masses of cars for import or export on the right.

Passing the mudflats of Bathside Bay, now being reclaimed to provide further space for the port to expand, we enter Dovercourt station, until recently graced by the suffix 'Bay' to denote the seaside attractions of the town. This is, to local people at least, the most important station on the line. It is then only a short ride to the passenger terminus at Harwich Town, where only one of the three platforms in used for its original purpose, the others being used to unload the car-carrying trains which make up a large proportion of the line's traffic. Even this is not quite the end of the line, for a short branch leads off northwards towards a train ferry berth a few hundred yards away. There is also a passenger ferry, more frequent in summer than in winter, across the estuary to Felixstowe.

COLCHESTER–CLACTON/WALTON
by Tony Baxter

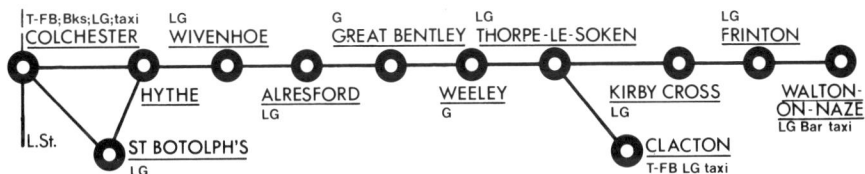

Low rainfall and long hours of sunshine coupled with excellent beaches have made the coastline of north-east Essex a popular holiday area. Walton had already begun to develop as a resort by the time that the Eastern Counties Railway reached Colchester in 1843. The opening in 1863 of the Tendring Hundred Railway from Colchester to Walton boosted its popularity and led to the development of neighbouring Frinton and Clacton later in the nineteenth century.

Leaving Colchester, our route diverges from the main line to Norwich a short distance from the North station and winds its way through the eastern outskirts of the town, giving glimpses of timber-framed buildings as a reminder of Colchester's historic past. At Eastgate, the line to the coast forms a triangular junction with the short branch to St. Botolph's station, served by quite frequent trains, and very conveniently situated in relation to the shopping centre and bus station. There are buses to such rail-less places as Mersea Island (half-hourly) and Halstead (hourly). Here may be seen a section of the town walls dating from the third century while nearby are the remains of St Botolph's Priory in which Roman bricks were re-used in the Norman structure. The branch was also constructed to serve the Colchester garrison, but an extension to the barracks, although authorised, was never built.

Returning to the main line to the coast, the train follows the north bank of the River Colne, past Colchester's Hythe docks, the highest point reached by ocean-

Seafront and pier, Clacton-on-Sea

going vessels. The towers of the University of Essex may be seen on the left on somewhat higher ground shortly before arriving at Wivenhoe. Here the station booking office still boasts a cast-iron fireplace incorporating the coat-of-arms of the Great Eastern Railway. Immediately opposite the station entrance a footpath leads down to the river where once a ferry plied across to Rowhedge on the opposite bank; now a six-mile detour by road is necessary. Also on the opposite bank and slightly further downstream is Fingringhoe nature reserve, worth a visit in winter to observe the bird life and in summer for the many rare and unusual wild flowers. A very infrequent bus service operates from Colchester to the village of Fingringhoe, about a mile from the nature reserve.

Wivenhoe declined in importance as a port with the deepening of the river to the Hythe in 1854; however, the miners' strike in 1984 resulted in an upsurge in traffic which has not since declined so that much heavy lorry traffic now uses the inadequate roads through the centre of the village. A possibility currently being investigated is to re-lay the railway track into the port area. Ship-building has been established here for over three centuries; recently it has also become a very popular yachting centre. Interesting walks may be taken along the river, both upstream towards the University and downstream towards Alresford Creek. Many species of bird may be seen, including heron and kingfisher, while large flocks of swans live in the vicinity. The village itself has a number of old houses including one with fine pargetting (decorated plasterwork).

Continuing our journey from Wivenhoe, we pass the trackbed of the Bright-lingsea branch (closed 1963) as the train climbs out of the river valley. Buses now run from Colchester to Brightlingsea every half hour, passing close to Alresford station, the next stop down the line. This is fruit farming country and vast orchards may be seen on either side of the line. However, there are still several areas of woodland, the last remnants of the forests which once covered much of Essex. Approaching Great Bentley, the twelfth-century church is clearly visible on the left, although the tower was not added until the fourteenth century. The station is one of the best kept on the line with a sunken ornamental garden surrounded by flower-beds.

The first indication that we are approaching a holiday area comes as we pass the caravan site at Weeley, set in pleasant woodland beside a lake. Shortly after, as the train slows for the Thorpe-le-Soken stop, a flying-saucer-like structure is just visible on the skyline to the right of the track; it is, in fact, an air traffic control beacon, an aid to aircraft navigation.

Thorpe-le-Soken is a busy junction station located a mile from the village it purports to serve. However, the very popular Monday market, held immediately outside the station, had been in existence many centuries before the trains came. When first constructed, the line continued only to Walton, but in 1882 a single track branch to Clacton was opened. Clacton gained rapidly in popularity in the early years of this century and the line was doubled soon after the opening of Butlin's Holiday Camp to cope with the very heavy summer Saturday holiday traffic. British Rail's presence was strengthened in 1981 with the opening of a £2-million electric traction maintenance depot adjacent to the station; prior to this, some work was carried out in the converted steam locomotive shed while other work had to be carried out elsewhere because of a lack of facilities.

Before leaving the station, pause a while to admire the flower stall, a magnificent display of blooms whatever the time of year, managed by an expert flower arranger. A short walk through the town centre, past the amusement arcades, brings us to the beach with its pier and sea front gardens topping low cliffs which stretch some two miles northwards to Holland-on-Sea. From the airfield, pleasure flights may be taken in summer over the surrounding countryside and along the coast towards Harwich and the Walton Backwaters. A frequent bus service (every fifteen minutes) runs to historic St Osyth; the priory was founded in the twelfth century but was later promoted to the status of an abbey. The superb flint flushwork gateway dates from the fifteenth century, while the house, built on the remains of the abbey, is Tudor.

Returning to Thorpe-le-Soken, the Walton train heads northwards along the single line past Kirby Cross, where there is a passing loop, and then, with the sea in view, towards Frinton. The station was opened in 1888 in response to the growing popularity of Frinton as a residential area, which became a select resort with tree-lined avenues and a broad greensward on the sea front. The appearance of the station has been much improved recently, as a result of the joint efforts of the station staff and the Frinton and Walton Heritage Trust, with carpeted waiting-rooms, flower-beds and a large mural on the disused platform (for a short time Frinton also had a passing loop) depicting the sea front in Edwardian times. In 1986, it was awarded a prize in the national competition for best kept stations.

Continuing towards Walton, the original route of the railway is clearly visible; in 1929 cliff erosion made it necessary to reconstruct this section of line further inland. At Walton, only one of the two original platforms remains in use while the locomotive depot has been converted into a coach-park. The station is situated on the cliff top less than a hundred yards from the beach which is the main attraction for the many thousands of visitors who come here every summer. In fact, the station buildings originally incorporated a bell-tower, the bell being rung to warn Victorian day-trippers on the beach below of the impending departure of their train. Now the whole station is scheduled to be rebuilt incorporating a block of flats on part of the site.

Walton pier accommodates the amusement arcades that one expects of any seaside pier, but the steamers which used to ply along the East Anglian coast, calling at Clacton as well as Walton, have long since gone. A short walk along the beach and the busy central area gives way to the wide open spaces of the Naze itself, a promontory now, alas, rapidly crumbling into the sea. Here is the Trinity House Tower, built in 1720 to aid navigation and within sight of the ports of Harwich and Felixstowe. Much cross-channel shipping can be observed; but for many visitors it is the bird life which they have come to see. Hundreds of sand-martins make their homes in the cliffs every summer while many other species may be observed both here and around the neighbouring backwaters. This was the setting Arthur Ransome chose for *Secret Water,* one of his 'Swallows and Amazons' books about a children's yachting holiday. The backwaters are also the home of the Walton and Frinton Yacht Club, one further attraction that brings visitors to this part of the Essex coast every summer.

STOUR VALLEY LINE
by Mike Davies

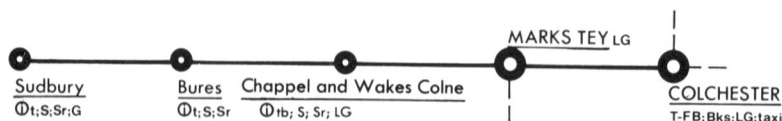

Sudbury	Bures	Chappel and Wakes Colne	MARKS TEY LG	COLCHESTER
①t;S;Sr;G	①t;S;Sr	①tb; S; Sr; LG		T-FB;Bks;LG;taxi

Background
With the coming of railways to East Anglia, the ancient and prosperous market town of Sudbury, 'Eatanswill' of *Pickwick Papers* and the birthplace of Thomas Gainsborough, was a natural choice for connection to the burgeoning rail network of Victorian England. The Colchester, Stour Valley & Halstead Railway duly opened to Sudbury with appropriate ceremony on 2 July 1849, reaching Cambridge on 1 June 1865 and Bury St Edmunds on 9 August 1865. The Beeching axe struck in the 1960s, leaving the original Marks Tey–Sudbury line as the truncated survivor of an extensive network of rural lines traversing the Essex–Suffolk border.

The journey–into the unknown
On joining the branch train at Marks Tey (reputedly the coldest station in Essex!), the traveller will immediately notice that the branch describes a sharp 90-degree curve, and in a few minutes the train is bearing away at right angles to the station platform into the delightfully rural and heavily wooded Essex uplands. Marks Tey once sported a refreshment room (latterly run by two ancient ladies who religiously locked the door whenever a train arrived!) and a fine Great Eastern station building adjacent to the overbridge at the north end. Now only a modern booking office and a fragment of the once extensive canopy remain.

The train is soon speeding down the side of the Colne Valley, curving around the line's principal engineering work: Chappel viaduct striding across the roofs of the village of the same name. This magnificent structure is 1,066 feet in length, has thirty-two arches, and achieves a height of seventy-five feet above the valley floor. Its construction consumed over seven million Suffolk white bricks. We grind to a halt in Chappel & Wales Colne station, once a busy junction with the independent Colne Valley Railway, a small concern linking Chappel and Haverhill

A Sprinter from Harwich crosses the River Stour en route to Ipswich (*Photo:* Nick Lewis)

with its own engineering works at Halstead, the headquarters of the line.

Chappel is now home to the East Anglian Railway Museum, an energetic body of enthusiasts who steam at least one of their vintage locomotives on regular open weekends throughout the summer. The buildings are being lovingly restored to their former glory by the museum. The imposing cast iron footbridge spanning the tracks was rescued from Sudbury station, restored and re-erected here.

Accelerating out of the station past sidings packed with a veritable Aladdin's cave of vintage stock on the right, an imposing signal-box and the old station pub (still with its engraved glass windows) on the left, we pass the junction with the Colne Valley Railway immediately below the road bridge. A solitary road bridge standing marooned in an orchard to the left bears silent testimony to the passing of a bustling little line. We press on through woods and leafy cuttings that form a green arch overhead in summer (watch out for deer, fox, and badgers here) and then, as the track dips away, we pick up speed and burst out into the Stour Valley, rattling down the side on a 1 in 90 incline which can prove daunting to the return service on a slippery autumn day.

A magnificent vista down the valley to the Vale of Dedham unfolds to the right. The imposing tower of Stoke-by-Nayland church stands sentinel on the far side, while to our left, as we rush towards Mount Bures level crossing, stands a wooded mound by the little church, reputedly the burial place of Boadicea; more recently the site of a fortified manor house.

We descend rapidly into Bures (pronounced Bu-ures), a compact village of great charm and many pubs nestling in the bottom of the valley, an ideal place to pause awhile to sample one of Greene King's potent brews of real East Anglian ale. On the far side stands a small chapel on St Edmund Hill where on Christmas Day AD 855 Edmund, saint and martyr, was crowned King of East Anglia.

On the final leg of its journey, the train keeps close to the river – which offers some of the finest fishing in East Anglia – and provides a grandstand view of some of the most attractive countryside of the Essex-Suffolk borders, once the stamping-ground of Thomas Gainsborough who recorded its every mood, and virtually unchanged to this day. Over the river, on an imposing iron bridge, the remains of a lock on the old Stour Valley Navigation can be seen through willow woods to the left. This ran from the quays of Sudbury to the sea at Harwich, transporting agricultural produce and the famous Ballingdon bricks (used in the construction of Liverpool Street station). Effectively killed off by the railway, it nevertheless lingered until the mid-1920s and there are long-term plans to re-open it to leisure traffic. Already one eighteenth-century canal warehouse at Sudbury has been restored to house the River Stour Trust and another is converted into a theatre.

Journey's end
And so to Sudbury, through the outskirts flanked by woods of willow and water-meadows. To the right is the large village of Cornard, now virtually part of Sudbury, where for several years there has been a campaign to provide it with a rail halt.

A sharp curve then brings us to the remains of Sudbury station, built when the line was extended to Cambridge, and used more recently as the Town Museum. This is overshadowed by the new Sudbury Kingfisher swimming-pool complex, designed to resemble a traditional Suffolk maltings in order to blend into the existing townscape. At the time of writing there are plans for a new rail terminus at Sudbury, as part of a supermarket development.

A short walk down the tree-lined station approach brings us to Market Hill, site of one of the largest open-air markets in the border country on Thursdays and Saturdays, when the town is alive with countryfolk.

An ancient town of charm and character, mixing Georgian and medieval architecture, and flanked by three imposing 'wool' churches, Sudbury is bounded on three sides by the Stour and water-meadows, common land held by the Freemen of the Borough since before the Norman Conquest. Visit Gainsborough's house and view his work before taking a stroll through history around the town. An excellent town trail guide is available from the Library – itself converted from the imposing Corn Exchange on Market Hill.

For the more adventurous, the line onwards from Sudbury is now a country trail ending at Rodbridge Corner, now a country park, but once the only level crossing in the country to be operated by a member of the Russian nobility! From here it is only a short step up the hill to the infamous Borley church, home of one of the best documented ghosts in the country. A local bus from the bus station (turn right at the end of the station approach), will take the traveller to Long Melford or Lavenham, both jewels in the crown of Suffolk, a county for which a trip up the Stour Valley Line makes a fitting start to a journey of discovery.

WITHAM–BRAINTREE
by Trevor Garrod

BRAINTREE   CRESSING   WHITE NOTLEY   WITHAM
G   L.St.   B;Bks;LG

Doctor Beeching wanted to close this 6¼-mile line in 1963. At that time, the service was operated by a diesel railbus seating fifty-six people.

Local users fought the closure proposal, won a reprieve and then, with remarkable support from the local council, set about promoting the service to boost patronage. Patient, steady work, including the twice-yearly distribution of publicity leaflets, brought results. A two-car diesel unit, seating 126 people, was needed in place of the railbus by the mid 1960s; then, in 1972, a three-car train providing 168 seats. In 1977 the line was electrified and it now enjoys a basic hourly service by four-car electric multiple units with some peak-hour through trains to and from Liverpool Street. It is not known whether the good Doctor ate his words before his death in 1985. . . .

The current custodians of the branch are the Witham & Braintree Rail Users' Association. They have campaigned successfully for the old Braintree station to be demolished and replaced by a modern building providing once again toilet and waiting-room facilities. The platforms will be able to take twelve-coach trains for the first time and work was expected to start in April 1989. The Association issues a pocket timetable showing the services available.

Witham is a busy junction station, branch line passengers departing from platform four. The town, dating back to the ninth century, has grown from 8,000 in 1958 to approximately 25,000 today. The station itself is built on the mound of the Anglo-Saxon fort.

The electric train leaves Witham station on a sharp curve, with a ten mph speed restriction, but is soon accelerating swiftly on the straight single track out into open country. It hugs the north side of the valley of the tiny River Brain, across which can be seen the red-brick Faulkbourne Hall in its park.

Three miles from Witham is White Notley station – rebuilt in 1977 to replace an old wooden structure. To the left, across the river, the village clusters round St Etheldreda's church with its white clapper-board bell-cote, typical of Essex.

Cressing station is vintage Great Eastern Railway and, like White Notley, is staffed by one man who also operates the crossing gates. It serves Cressing and Black Notley, two villages with much modern housing, on opposite sides of the valley which now narrows as we see Braintree ahead, dominated by the spire of St Michael's church.

Before reaching the town the line passes over the new Braintree bypass, then a golf-course on the left and a factory on the right with UKF Fertilisers freight sidings, before the train swings round a curve to enter Braintree station. Next to it are car-parks whose area has expanded as the service has grown in popularity.

This railway reached Braintree in 1848, and was extended to Bishops Stortford in 1869. By 1966, the western section had closed completely. The ancient town of Braintree developed silk and engineering industries and, nowadays, also attracts London commuters. A short walk from the station is the busy market-place, a good range of shops, eating- and drinking-places, and the Old Town Hall which now contains an arts centre and a display of local history. Close by is the bus station whose services include a half-hourly one to Halstead and less frequent ones to Castle Hedingham, Great Bardfield and the showpiece village of Finchingfield.

Electric train on Braintree branch

SOME MAJOR CITIES AND TOWNS

NORWICH
by Louis Hipperson

The capital of East Anglia has been a place of importance for over a thousand years. At the time of the Norman Conquest, it was one of the largest towns in England and was a market centre serving east Norfolk, then the most densely populated part of the country. This early status of Norwich was reflected in the building of a royal castle shortly after 1066 and in the start of a cathedral in 1096. The cathedral spire is the second highest in England (315 feet).

The medieval period was, in general, a time of great prosperity for the city. Its wealth was based on foreign trade carried on through its port and the multiplicity of crafts practised by its inhabitants. Throughout the Middle Ages Norwich was the second or third city of England, its only rivals being Bristol and York. Tax returns suggest that in 1662, Norwich was probably the country's largest provincial town.

The city's lack of easy access to the essential raw materials of the industrial revolution caused a decline in its ranking, gradual at first so that in 1801 it was still England's third city, but by 1861 its population was exceeded by that of many Midland and northern towns.

Today Norwich is noted for the manufacture of footwear, food and drink, printing and bookbinding, engineering, chemical technology, clothing, banking, and insurance. The last has developed world-wide connections. Since the Second World War, Her Majesty's Stationery Office has moved its headquarters to the city.

Visitors by rail to Norwich can reach the centre by boarding a minibus in the station forecourt. Departures are every few minutes throughout the day until early evening.

The present population of Norwich is about 120,000, with more than 60,000 in the extensive outer suburbs beyond the present city boundaries. Norwich has a vast hinterland, embracing most of Norfolk and much of north Suffolk. This explains why it has considerably more shops than many places of similar size. The shops range from large department stores to small premises serving a wide variety of special requirements.

The most striking witness to Norwich's importance and wealth in the medieval period lies in the pre-Reformation churches within the walled central area. Originally there were more than fifty; the thirty-two that remain are mostly of the Perpendicular period. It is now claimed that this number is not exceeded in any other city in Europe.

Among other buildings of interest are the large Roman Catholic cathedral of St John the Baptist (1894–1910) and the twentieth-century brick and stone City Hall (note the Swedish influence). The latter overlooks the market-place, occupied by the stalls of an open-air provision and general goods market, one of the largest in the country.

Norwich has a rich cultural life. The castle (whose stone keep was drastically restored in 1834) houses a museum and art galleries. The latter contain works of the Norwich School of Painters. The city has several other museums a large central library (with an excellent local studies' department), and a number of theatres (including the world-famous Maddermarket). Many opportunities exist for hearing good music. The University of East Anglia, occupying an open site on the city's western edge, was founded in 1963.

Among other outstanding aspects of this fascinating city are the many open spaces comprising parks, gardens and two riverside walks. Professional football is played at Carrow Road and minor counties cricket at Lakenham. And who has not heard of the Norwich terrier and the Norwich canary?

More detailed information on the city is available at the tourist information centre housed in the fifteenth-century flint-faced Guildhall next to the market-place.

CAMBRIDGE
by Geoffrey Roper

The national – indeed international – fame of Cambridge rests on its university and colleges, but for the city itself they have sometimes been a mixed blessing. It was they, for instance, who insisted on the elegantly arcaded railway station being built (in 1845) more than a mile from the city centre. Nevertheless, it is the architectural splendours of the colleges which the rail-borne visitor comes chiefly to see, and so he or she must take the bus (frequent services from outside the station), or join the throngs of cyclists for which Cambridge is renowned.

From the centre, the historic colleges and university buildings are all within easy walking distance. The tourist information centre in Wheeler Street, behind the Guildhall, provides maps and guides and, if required, can arrange conducted tours and book overnight accommodation.

The earliest settlement of Cambridge, in Roman times, was to the north-west on the other side of the River Cam in the area of the castle (now just a grassy mound in the grounds of the Shire Hall). This was followed by an Anglo-Saxon village which gradually spread southwards across the river. By the twelfth century, the present centre and the basic layout of the town was established, with its two main arteries converging at the Norman round church in Bridge Street, and the market-place lying between them a little further to the south.

In 1201 the first charter was granted to what was by then a thriving market town, and later that century the university came into being. The oldest college is Peterhouse, founded in 1280, and there are fifteen others of the medieval and Tudor periods. All have buildings of great architectural and historical interest, ranging from the famous cathedral-like chapel of King's to the remarkable Pepys Library (complete with all the books and bookcases of the famous seventeenth-century diarist) at Magdalene. Most colleges are normally open to visitors during the daytime, except in May and June (because of examinations).

Seven of these old colleges are adjacent to the river, and the area to their rear, with lawns, willow trees, gardens, and little bridges, known as the Backs, has been described as 'the most perfect man-made view in England'. In the summer, punts may be hired to enjoy this view to the best effect.

The university itself, although historically less important than the colleges, has interesting medieval and later buildings, notably the group known as the Old Schools, with the eighteenth-century Senate House, opposite the magnificent University Church of Great St Mary (whose tower offers a good view over the roof-tops of the town). The important and sometimes controversial nineteenth- and twentieth-century architecture of both university and colleges should not be ignored.

A walk round the city will also reveal many interesting non-university buildings, old and new, among them a number of fine medieval and later churches, the massive high Victorian Corn Exchange, now a concert hall, opposite the tourist information centre, and the splendid late Victorian building of Foster's (now

Lloyd's) Bank, on the corner of Sidney Street and Hobson Street. The exploring visitor will also quickly become aware of the extensive green open spaces and commons which are one of the features of Cambridge.

The attractive and historic villages of Trumpington, Grantchester (famous for its association with Rupert Brooke), Fen Ditton, Coton, and Histon are within easy reach. The last-named still has a railway and station building on the Cambridge to St Ives freight branch which many residents and visitors would like to see reopened for passengers; this would also help ease the congestion caused by commuters' cars in the city.

Back in the city, it remains to mention the museums and art galleries, including the world-famous Fitzwilliam Museum in Trumpington Street, the Cambridge and County Folk Museum in Castle Street, and a number of specialised scientific and archaeological museums maintained by the university departments. Full details and opening times can be found in *A Brief Guide to Museums in Cambridgeshire*, obtainable at the tourist information centre.

Cambridge is an important shopping centre, with several department stores, a flourishing daily market, many specialised small shops and one of the country's largest bookshops (Heffer's in Trinity Street). All in all, Cambridge offers so much to see and do, that a day trip can only whet the appetite for a more extended visit.

IPSWICH
by Alan Cocker

Your impending arrival at Ipswich by train is marked from the south by a view of the docks, while from the north the towers of Sproughton sugar-beet factory are a sign of home to inhabitants of Suffolk's county town. This is fitting, for much of the prosperity of Ipswich past and present has been built on its port and in supplying the support industries for the surrounding agricultural area.

A settlement has existed here for well over a thousand years, so the visitor may be surprised that Ipswich is not more obviously 'historical'. The Ancient House seems almost the only historical attraction. The truth is that the treasures of Ipswich's past take a little finding, partly because they are often off the beaten track (such as the Unitarian Meeting House in Lower Brook Street and the Custom House), and partly because they seem overwhelmed by modern life. Thus a visit to the tourist information centre in the Town Hall is recommended before exploring old Ipswich.

To escape the bustle, visit Christchurch Park near the town centre. It is one of a number of extensive parks within the borough and contains the Elizabethan mansion which is open to the public and is well worth seeing.

If you have time, you may appreciate the recently pedestrianised shopping centre, the Wolsey Theatre and Corn Exchange entertainments complex. There are also extensive sports facilities in both town and suburbs.

COLCHESTER
by Lewis Buckingham

Situated on the River Colne, fifty-two miles by rail from London, Colchester is Britain's oldest recorded town. The main North station, about one mile from the town centre, is connected to it by frequent buses and also by half-hourly daytime local trains on weekdays to the conveniently situated St Botolph's station, which itself has an hourly service to the coastal resorts of Clacton-on-Sea, Frinton-on-

Sea, and Walton-on-Naze. St Botolph's is also served by some Sudbury branch line trains.

Camulodunum, as Colchester was known in ancient times, has a history stretching back long before the Roman invasion in AD 43. The first Roman city was founded here and, although destroyed by Queen Boadicea in AD 61, was rebuilt to become a walled city and the most important Roman centre in Britain. Parts of the wall still stand, including the ruined Balkerne Gateway. The eleventh-century Norman castle, built on the foundations of a Roman temple, has the largest keep in Europe, and is now a museum in an attractive park.

Today's Colchester is a thriving town with a busy port. There are many fine stores, supermarkets, and new shopping precincts. There are five museums: Hollytrees (customs and antiquities), Holy Trinity (social history), All Saints (natural history), Tymperleys Clock Museum (open April to October), as well as the castle and the Minories Art Gallery. Together with the medieval churches, a modern sports centre, a Dutch quarter where the Flemish weavers originally settled, these buildings provide a pleasing mixture of ancient and modern.

The Town Hall with its fine clock-tower was completed in 1902, and it is there in the Moot Hall that the annual oyster feast is held. The 'natives' (oysters) have been famous since Roman times.

Standing in the shadow of 'Jumbo' (the Victorian water-tower, no longer in use), the Mercury Theatre provides entertainment throughout the year.

During the summer months, a sightseeing tour by open-top bus is available. Dedham, in the heart of Constable country, is easily reached by bus as are Colchester Zoo and many attractive villages, while the coast is easily accessible by rail and bus.

LOWESTOFT
by Trevor Garrod

Lowestoft's growth in the nineteenth century from a large fishing village to a sizeable town (population now over 60,000) was due mainly to the railway and its associated docks. The station is thus well-sited for the fish dock (not open to the public but guided tours are available to organised groups), the pedestrianised main street and recently-opened Britten Centre with its growing range of shops and adjacent bus station.

Just to the south of the railway is Lake Lothing – the inlet which cuts the town in two and serves as a commercial harbour. Immediately beyond the bascule bridge is the remarkable building of the Royal Norfolk and Suffolk Yacht Club, the yacht basin, and then two miles of sandy beach – awarded the EEC Blue Flag for cleanliness in 1989 – with two piers and a good range of public gardens and amusements, backed by solid and stately Victorian terraces built in the town's heyday as a fashionable 'watering place'. On this lively stretch of beach, during the season, will be found Punch and Judy, trampolines, and life-guards; while sea front attractions include putting-green, boating-lake, crazy golf, and tourist information centre – all within a few minutes' walk of the station.

A mile to the north of the modern centre is the old High Street, leading to the lighthouse, Belle Vue Park (naval memorial), and Sparrow's Nest (maritime museum). On the northern edge of the town are Pleasurewood Hills Leisure Park, on the bus route to Yarmouth via Corton (service 603) and a nudist beach.

There is a town map in Station Square, while town buses and minibuses can be caught just round the corner in Waveney Road. For nearby Oulton Broad there are also buses – but many visitors and local people prefer the five-minute train journey to one of its two stations.

FOR FURTHER READING AND REFERENCE

BOOKS

The East Anglia Tourist Board (Toppesfield Hall, Hadleigh, Ipswich, Suffolk IP7 5DN) publishes a cheap but comprehensive annual guide that gives information on what to see and do in Essex, Cambridgeshire, Norfolk and Suffolk. It gives descriptions, opening times and admission prices of places to visit. The Board also produces information sheets and leaflets, many of them free.

Books that deal with East Anglia – either in general or on specific topics – are legion. Your local public library may have suitable material in stock. Otherwise, if requested, staff will try to obtain items for you through the inter-library lending scheme. Public libraries can also give advice on publishing details and prices, and say if books are in print.

Works concerned wholly or partly with the history of East Anglian railways include:

Allen, Ian C. *55 years of East Anglian steam*. Oxford Publishing Co., 1982.

Brodribb, John *Steam in the eastern counties*. Ian Allan, 1985.

Brodribb, John *LNER Country Stations*. Ian Allan, 1988.

Gordon, D. I. *A regional history of the railways of Great Britain*, vol. 5: *The eastern counties*. 2nd edition, David & Charles, 1977.

Joby, R. S. *Forgotten railways of East Anglia*, 2nd revised edition, David St John Thomas, 1985, (Deals with dismantled lines.)

Simmons, Jack *The railways of Britain: an historical introduction* 2nd edition. Macmillan, 1968 (Contents include 'a complete analysis of the railway system in a single county, Suffolk').

Swinger, Peter W. *East Anglia*. David & Charles, 1983. (Railway history in pictures).

MAPS

Ordnance Survey publishes maps of various scales, each series for particular purposes. For further details write to Information and Public Enquiries, Ordnance Survey, Romsey Road, Maybush, Southampton SO9 4DH.

Bartholomew: the following maps in the National Map Series (5/8th inch to 1 mile) embrace the area covered by this book: 16 – Essex; 20 – Cambridgeshire (except Fens); 21 – Suffolk; 25 – Fenland; 26 – Norfolk. Further particulars from John Bartholomew & Sons, Duncan Street, Edinburgh EH9 1TA.

TOWN STREET PLANS

G. I. Barnett & Son Ltd, Rippleside Commercial Estate, Ripple Road, Barking, Essex IG11 0SB (many East Anglian towns);

Colour Maps International, 145 Crostwick Lane, Spixworth, Norwich NR10 3NG (a few towns in Norfolk and Suffolk);

Mr Wilfrid George, 43 Linden Road, Aldeburgh, Suffolk IP15 5JH (drawer and publisher). (Certain towns and rural areas in Norfolk, Suffolk and north Essex). Mr George also publishes maps of rural footpaths. Some plans are the most up-to-date available, but it is essential to use these in conjunction with an Ordnance Survey map, preferably the Pathfinder series (2½" to 1 mile).

Jarrold Colour Publications, Norwich, publish a wide range of pictorial guides of East Anglia and the Broads, and also the most definitive maps of Norwich.

TIMETABLES AND LEAFLETS

British Rail publish a Passenger Timetable of over 1,200 pages for the whole country, issued in May and October each year and on sale at staffed stations and booksellers. Timetable booklets are also published for groups of lines, sometimes at a small charge; while pocket-sized timetable leaflets are also obtainable, free, for individual lines, as are leaflets on taking bicycles by train.

Suffolk County Council's footpath maps and guides can be obtained from libraries or from the County Planning Department, St Edmund House, Rope Walk, Ipswich, Suffolk IP4 1LZ.

BUSES

Bus deregulation introduced under the 1986 Transport Act means that information about services can quickly become out of date. We cannot therefore accept any responsibility for such information, but recommend that you seek the latest details by phoning the relevant County Council bus inquiry number:

Bedfordshire: 0234 228337	Cambridgeshire: 0223 317740
Essex 0245 352232	Hertfordshire 0992 556765
Suffolk 0473 230000	Norfolk 0603 613613

For Norfolk you can also call in at, or write to, NORBIC (Norfolk Bus Information Centre), 4 Guildhall Hill, Norwich NR2 1JH.

Note that most numbers are only available during office hours. Information can also be obtained from any Network SouthEast travel centre (except Ely) and from *Doe's bus/rail guide* which gives information about services between railheads and principal non rail-served destinations throughout the country.

Doe's bus/rail guide is obtainable at £4 (post free) from B. S. Doe, 25 Newmorton Road, Moordown, Bournemouth, Dorset BH9 3NU. The latest edition at the time of writing includes every town of over 7000 population not served by rail and many smaller centres as well. Indications of bus frequency, first and last bus of the day, and location of bus-stop nearest the station, are included.

Also available from the same address is *Doe's directory of bus timetables* which lists bus operators on a county-by-county basis and costs £2.

MARKET DAYS

Knowledge of these may help you plan your journeys in the more rural areas, since many towns have extra buses on market days:

Mondays: St Ives, Aylsham

Tuesdays: Saffron Walden, Hitchin, Newmarket, Halstead, Ipswich, Spalding, King's Lynn

Wednesdays: Royston, Bury, Braintree, Saxmundham, March, Watton

Thursdays: St Neots, Bishops Stortford, Ely, Sudbury, Stowmarket, Woodbridge, Wisbech, Oundle, Fakenham

Fridays: Haverhill, Mildenhall, Diss, Stamford, Downham Market, Beccles, East Dereham

Saturdays: Huntingdon, Thetford, Swaffham

WHAT IS THE RAILWAY DEVELOPMENT SOCIETY?

The Railway Development Society is the national voluntary independent body which campaigns for better rail services, for both passengers and freight, and greater use of rail transport.

It publishes books and reports, holds meetings and exhibitions, sometimes runs special trains, and puts the rail users' point of view to politicians, commerce, and industry as well as referring users' comments and suggestions to British Rail management and unions.

There are fifteen branches of the Society covering all of Great Britain. The East Anglian Branch covers the region described in this book. Affiliated to the Society are a growing number of rail users' associations which campaign for particular lines, stations, or groups of stations. Together with these local associations, the Society aims to provide a nationwide voice for rail users.

Membership is open to all who are in general agreement with the aims of the Society and subscriptions (as at April 1989) are:

Standard rate: **£7.50**

Pensioners, students, unemployed: **£4.00**

Families: **£7.50** plus £1.00 for each member of household

The Membership Secretary is Mr. F. J. Hastilow, 49 Irnham Road, Sutton Coldfield, West Midlands B74 2TQ.

For other information about the Society, write to the General Secretary, Mr T. J. Garrod, 15 Clapham Road, Lowestoft, Suffolk NR32 1RQ. For information about the East Anglian Branch, write to the Secretary, Mr P. R. Lawrence, 75 Marlpit Lane, Norwich NR5 8XN

Local rail users' associations affiliated to the Railway Development Society (many of whom also concern themselves with local bus services) are:

East Norfolk Travellers' Association: Secretary – Peter Warner, 57 Clarkson Road, Lingwood, Norwich, Norfolk.

East Suffolk Travellers' Association: Secretary – John Brodribb, 12 Kemps Lane, Beccles, Suffolk NR34 9XA.

East Suffolk Travellers' Association (Felixstowe): Secretary – Charles Taylor, 15 Gainsborough Road, Felixstowe, Suffolk IP11 7HT.

Fen Line Users' Association: Secretary – Stuart Todd, 19 Hall Road, King's Lynn, Norfolk PE30 3DD.

North East Norfolk Travellers' Association: Secretary – Ray Davies, 10 Buxton Road, North Walsham, Norfolk NR28 0EU.

Sudbury–Marks Tey Rail Users' Association: Chairman – Mike Davies, 45 Elm Road, Sudbury, Suffolk.

Walton, Frinton & Kirby Rail Users' Group: Secretary – Ewan Lake, 3 Eton Road, Frinton-on-Sea, Essex CO13 9JA.

Witham–Braintree Rail Users' Association: Chairman – David Bigg, Eye-level, 76 Maldon Road, Witham, Essex.

ISBN 0-7117-0433-3
© Railway Development Society 1985, 1989
Published by Jarrold Colour Publications, Norwich
Printed in Great Britain 3/89